PROMISE KEEPERS®
MEN OF INTEGRITY

PROMISE BUILDERS™
— STUDY SERIES —

APPLYING
THE
SEVEN PROMISES

PUBLISHING
Colorado Springs, Colorado

To contact the authors, write: Marketplace Connections
                               1800 30th Street
                               Suite 219
                               Boulder, CO 80301

CONTENTS

FOREWORD

We live in an age of moral relativism. Our society says it really doesn't matter what you do as long as *you* believe in it–and don't restrict others from doing the same. A world devoid of absolutes is the logical consequence of a generation that has forgotten or denied the existence of a living, personal God.

But the Spirit of God is stirring men across our nation to hunger for truth. Man by man, He reveals the void within our hearts designed to be filled by God alone. This is a very good thing. For as Jesus promised, "Blessed are those who hunger and thirst for righteousness, for they will be filled" (Matt. 5:6).

Ron Ralston, Bob Horner, and David Sunde recognized in the men around them the growing desire to learn more of God and His ways. They presented to Promise Keepers a format and grid for Bible studies based on their experience–collectively, over 100 years of discipling others. As we evaluated their model, we found that it paralleled the approach that has evolved in Promise Keepers. We envisioned, along with them, a short, simple format that didn't require extensive homework. We agreed that the studies should provide a common ground for men to study together what God says about His standards in Scripture and, more than that, discover together what they could do to keep their promises, not just make them.

We've adapted this Bible study model to consider the *Seven Promises of a Promise Keeper* and to facilitate increasing participation by members of the group. You'll find that these 45 weeks of study take you through not only various promises, but also the relational progress of a small group– going from the acquaintance stage to the encouragement stage, and hopefully to the brother-to-brother stage.

The following pages contain a simple, profound, and methodical approach to studying God's Word and His standards with your brothers in Christ. I encourage you to dive in so that we might become the generation that unashamedly raises God's standards in word and Living Word, that we might be a godly influence in our world.

Pete Richardson
VP Communication Services
Promise Keepers

ACKNOWLEDGMENTS

First and foremost, we give all the glory to our Lord, Jesus Christ.

This Promise Builders small group study is the result of many talented individuals who pooled their skills and resources. We would like to recognize the following for their faithfulness:

- Bob Horner, Ron Ralston, and David Sunde, all from Marketplace Connections with Campus Crusade for Christ International, who wrote the studies.

- Larry Weeden with Focus on the Family, who edited the studies.

- Rob Johnson with Wilson-Johnson Creative for the cover design.

- Larry Thompson, Sherry Thompson, and Laura Stowers with Thompson & Thompson for the content design and layout.

- Pete Richardson, VP Communication Services; Jim Gordon, Manager of Publications; and Susie Swenson, Project Coordinator from Promise Keepers, who coordinated this project from original concept to the finished printed books.

The entire team is excited about the many ways God will work through you as you work through these studies.

INTRODUCTION

A sign of growth in the world of nature is change—change in the dimensions of a tree, fruit appearing on the vine, and flowers blooming in the garden. In a similar way, change for us means new levels of maturity, of understanding, and in the way we relate to our family and friends—truly being a Promise Keeper. But what does it take for change to occur? In one word, time. Not just the ticking of the clock, but time that is given purposefully in this next year to study God's Word with brothers in Christ and become accountable to each other. Your life will be re-engineered week by week in the hour you invest in the group. The goal is not to make you a Bible scholar, but to help you learn to live with Jesus Christ as the center of your life, one day at a time.

This book contains 45 sessions of Bible studies for your small group—a year's supply. It is anticipated that your group will meet weekly except for unforeseen situations unique to your group. As well, the 45 sessions include special studies planned for Thanksgiving, the Christmas season, the New Year (two sessions), and Easter, located on pages 96-103. Each weekly session is designed to take one hour.

The questions for each session are answered interactively in the group. Open with fellowship around coffee and friendship, then allow 40 minutes to interact with the biblical material. Use the final 10 minutes for application and prayer. A special Prayer Journal is provided to record the various requests week by week.

This may be your first time to participate in a weekly small group that meets for fellowship, Bible study, and prayer. Some men are hesitant to get involved simply because they're not sure where the group is going. In this case, we're seeking to take the next step from the stadium to the small group. We believe that when men gather in the name of Jesus Christ, Almighty God is pleased. And when they gather weekly to fellowship, pray, and apply God's Word, measurable change takes place. So call your friends. Pick a place to meet, and go for it!

"Be on your guard; stand firm in the faith; be men of courage; be strong. Do everything in love" (1 Cor. 16:13).

Bob Horner
Ron Ralston
David Sunde

THE BEST APPROACH FOR YOUR GROUP

AN OVERVIEW TO SEVERAL PATTERNS OF MEN'S SMALL-GROUP BIBLE STUDIES

Men who gather in a small group to fellowship, study the Bible, and pray together predictably follow one of several patterns. Often they aren't even aware of what their group has become, since they're accustomed to it. Of course, the leader of the group has tremendous influence in this area. The kind of group we have in mind for these sessions may call for some changes in the way you do things (if yours is an established group). But we hope you'll see the benefits of becoming a group that majors on interactive discussion and application of the timeless insights of God's Word.

" Adrift"—The Life Raft Group.

This small group is made up of survivors—men who have survived a major battle in their lives. It may have been a recent battle or one from years ago. But the wounds and scars are reminders of what each has suffered. What began as an emergency situation has turned into a weekly meeting. So each man is just happy to be among his friends. Life raft groups really have no leader—each man has his own story to tell around some biblical idea or paragraph. Of concern to the men is that they're adrift. And though high on encouragement, they're low on long-term biblical resources.

"Feeling Good"—The Yacht Group.

If you long to feel good among friends, climb aboard this craft! The skipper will welcome you with a hot cup of coffee or whatever else you'd like. Each man needs a Bible, of course—and the study will begin as soon as they push off. But meanwhile, just enjoy the Lord and each other. For some reason, the seagoing stories of fellow mariners always take more time than the skipper planned for, so time in the Word will resume next week. Your need to move beyond the fellowship—to get into the Word—may urge you on to see what other boats are in the harbor.

"Battle Weary"—The Destroyer Group.

This pattern is named after the naval vessel of the same class. It's a warship, armed and ready for battle against the forces of

vil in society and our lives.
isciplined Bible study is the order of
ie day. Truth from Scripture is fired
om the leader like missiles from the
eck launchers. Some of the sailors
ok as if they took direct hits from
ie Word, but the leader has properly
arned them that such are the costs of
iscipleship. No one questions the
ality of spiritual warfare, though the
attle-weary men sense the need for
me spiritual support from the Lord.

**Deep and Long: Where Are We?"—
The Submarine
Group.** To the captain
of the sub, there are
just two kinds of boats:
subs and targets.
Aboard this kind of
small group, Bible study
ves the experience of going down
eep, staying down long, and, after a
hile, wondering where you really are.
life of disciplined study is essential if
ou're to last with this group. And
ou may not be sure the captain likes
ou, but you know you're investing
me in a highly strategic activity,
elow the surface of life. If it's fellow-
ip balanced with interactive Bible
udy and prayer you're looking for,
owever, you'd better not go down the

ladder into the sub group.

**"Refreshed, Refueled, Refocused"—
The Carrier
Group.** An aircraft
carrier is a warship
equipped with a
large open deck for
the taking off and
landing of warplanes. As well, it's
equipped to carry, service, and arm its
planes. A small group Bible study in
this pattern is on a mission, underway
to be in strategic position for the men
on board. Each time the men come in,
in the midst of the work week, they
know they will be refreshed, refueled,
and refocused for life's battles and
open seas. They leave ready to fulfill
the biblical plan they studied, alert to
serve their Captain well. This kind of
small group is what we have in mind
for the sessions ahead. Of course
there is value in the other kinds of
group patterns, but we believe that the
aircraft carrier model best serves our
goal of becoming Promise Builders in
the year before us.

LEADER'S GUIDELINES

Leaders of small-group Bible studies have traditionally been people of superior biblical knowledge and (hopefully) great spiritual maturity. But in Promise Builders small groups, we're changing some of the rules. Our leaders are meant to be facilitators, not biblical experts. The purpose of the Promise Builder group leader is to encourage discussion and interaction. Thus, he is more a coach than a commentator. In other words, the group is meant to be leader-light.

There are, however, a few other responsibilities for the leader:

• Start and end each session on time. This shows respect for the men and their duties.

• Pray for group members by name before each meeting.

• Value each man's comments and insights.

• No matter where you start in the calendar year, be aware of the special sessions for seasonal holidays.

• The meeting can take place most anywhere, but we suggest a room like the back of a restaurant, a cafeteria, a conference room, a community center, or someone's office.

• Work closely with the men who are facilitating the group in other ways, such as the timekeepers, the prayer leader, and the calendar coordinato

Following these simple guidelines, plus the carrier-group mindset described earlier and the session gam plan given in "Group Guidelines," will help you and the other men in your group to see life-changing results as you go through the studies in this book.

GROUP GUIDELINES

Promise Builders groups are esigned to harness the mighty omentum and excitement of the assive stadium events of a Promise eepers weekend. Each session of the llow-through small group has been ritten with the seven promises of Promise Keeper in mind. In fact, ich session focuses on and seeks to it into practice one of the seven omises. That way, the promises ecome life-changing, in the power the Holy Spirit.

Through these sessions, your oup will discover biblically based sights in the context of the seven omises. It's important that these udies be done as a group. We're not omoting spiritual Lone Rangers. ather, we seek to build the Body of hrist as we meet together in a group tting.

To help you accomplish your jectives, we suggest this plan for ich session:

pening 10 minutes: socializing and fellowship

ain 40 minutes: Bible study in a seven promises context

Final 10 minutes: writing prayer requests in the Prayer Journal at the back of this book and praying together.

The Relational Diamond

Friends
Encourage

Brothers
Exhort

Acquaintances
Accept

Christlike

The process of building vital relationships among men can be likened to a baseball diamond. There are four phases of development you will encounter as you strive toward maturity.

The process starts as we step up to the plate with the desire and determination to become more like Christ. As we head toward first base and begin to accept one another, men develop acquaintances with each other. On the way to second base, the relationships progress to the level of friendship as we encourage one another. From second to third, we move deeper into each other's lives, allowing us to exhort one another. From there, we round third base and head toward home plate, committed to becoming the brothers Jesus intends us to be.

With the help of the Holy Spirit, you should without fear be able to go around the bases of mature Christian love.

Each session in this year-long study is intended to help you and your group advance around the bases. But it may take longer than a year to achieve the levels of friendship suggested by the relational diamond. In other words, you may end the year of sessions together just rounding second base—getting closer as brothers, for sure, but not yet ready to head for home plate. And that's okay. The main thing is that you're advancing; you're not where you started as the year began.

Our challenge to you is to stay together as a group for a second year of studying God's Word. To help you achieve that goal, Promise Keepers has prepared a second year of interactive Bible study sessions especially for small groups like yours. That way, you will continue to grow in your relationships with each other. The goal of becoming Christlike brothers will be much closer as together you head for home plate.

MISSION STATEMENT

Promise Keepers is a Christ-centered ministry dedicated to uniting men through vital relationships to become godly influences in their world.

THE SEVEN PROMISES
OF A PROMISE KEEPER

1 **A man and his God.**
A Promise Keeper is committed to honoring Jesus Christ through worship, prayer, and obedience to God's Word in the power of the Holy Spirit.

2 **A man and his friends.**
A Promise Keeper is committed to pursuing vital relationships with a few other men, understanding that he needs brothers to help him keep his promises.

3 **A man and his integrity.**
A Promise Keeper is committed to practicing spiritual, moral, ethical, and sexual purity.

4 **A man and his family.**
A Promise Keeper is committed to building strong marriages and families through love, protection, and biblical values.

5 **A man and his church.**
A Promise Keeper is committed to supporting the mission of his church by honoring and praying for his pastors and by actively giving his time and resources.

6 **A man and his brothers.**
A Promise Keeper is committed to reaching beyond any racial and denominational barriers to demonstrate the power of biblical unity.

7 **A man and his world.**
A Promise Keeper is committed to influencing his world, being obedient to the Great Commandment (see Mark 12:30-31) and the Great Commission (see Matt. 28:19-20).

No Man Is an Island

• •

WARM-UP:

LOOKING BACK OVER THE LAST TWO TO THREE YEARS, WHAT ARE THE MOST MEMORABLE TIMES YOU RECALL WITH A SMALL GROUP OF MEN? WHY?

BOB WAS SURPRISED AT WHAT A GOOD TIME HE HAD TRAVELING TO A PROMISE KEEPERS CONFERENCE WITH A VAN LOAD OF GUYS. HOWEVER, AS ENJOYABLE AS THAT TIME WAS, HE WAS RELUCTANT TO MOVE FROM THE MOMENTUM OF THE STADIUM TO A SMALL MEN'S GROUP. WHAT CAN YOU SAY TO ENCOURAGE BOB TO BE PART OF THIS GROUP?

BACKGROUND

Our experience at a Promise Keepers conference has taught us that there is value in being together as men. Solomon, who was given great wisdom from God, has much to say to us on the subject.

READ

ECCLESIASTES 4:9–13

QUESTIONS FOR INTERACTION:

1 What life principles does Solomon impart that teach us the importance of being together?

2 Two hunters are lost in the Rockies. How would Solomon advise them about their chances of survival together versus being lost alone?

3 What pressures of work and home do most men deal with in order to survive?

4 In light of this passage, what are some things we can expect from this small group?

5 Why might some men not feel the need for a group? (v. 13)

WRAP-UP: ON A 3x5 CARD, WRITE THE NUMBERS ONE TO FOUR. NEXT TO EACH NUMBER, WRITE DOWN A PRAYER REQUEST IN THE FOLLOWING AREAS:

1. PERSONAL
2. IN RELATIONSHIP WITH GOD
3. FAMILY
4. WORK

• •

PROMISE 2: A MAN AND HIS FRIENDS

MY RESPONSE AS A PROMISE KEEPER

Exchange 3x5 cards and pray for that one person during the week.

HOW LONG CAN YOU TREAD WATER?

● ●

WARM-UP: FOR SOME, "RISKY" IS LOSING YOUR JOB AT AGE 45, WALKING TO A CORNER MARKET IN THE INNER CITY, SKIING OFF A CORNICE, GIVING A REPORT BEFORE YOUR PEERS, OR BEING ADMITTED TO THE HOSPITAL. FOR OTHERS, JUST TELLING THEIR COLLEAGUES THEIR GOLF SCORE IS SCARY ENOUGH.

WHAT'S THE RISKIEST THING YOU CAN REMEMBER DOING? WHY DID YOU DO IT?

BACKGROUND

After seeing Jesus feed 5,000 men with a kid's sack lunch, Peter must have emerged with a great deal of confidence in his Lord's ability to provide in every imaginable situation. Within a few hours, however, Jesus asked Peter to do something he had never done before – in fact, something so risky that Peter would never have tried it unless the Lord Himself directed him to it.

READ

 MATTHEW 14:22–33

QUESTIONS FOR INTERACTION:

1 For a fisherman, his boat is everything. Why do you think Jesus called Peter out of his boat?

2 Why did Peter do it?

3 What do you think went through Peter's mind while walking on the water?

4 Why does the Lord often push us into risky situations?

5 What caused this confident water-walker to start swallowing seawater?

6 What might Peter have learned about Jesus here?

7 What would you like to learn about Jesus in a group like this?

WRAP-UP: PETER, WHEN OVERWHELMED BY HIS FEAR, UTTERED THE SHORTEST PRAYER IN THE BIBLE. IN LIGHT OF A RISKY SITUATION AHEAD, EACH MAN SAY HOW HE WOULD LIKE THE GROUP TO PRAY FOR HIM.

● ●

PROMISE 1: A MAN AND HIS GOD

MY RESPONSE AS A PROMISE KEEPER

In light of a current risky situation, I will choose to look at Jesus instead of the "waves."

I will commit to tell this group next week how my faith has been strengthened.

MR. GoodSoil

P R O M I S E   5 :   A   M A N   A N D   H I S   C H U R C H

WARM-UP: EVERYONE WOULD LIKE TO HAVE MORE MONEY AND TIME. WE DREAM OF WINNING A MULTIMILLION-DOLLAR LOTTO JACKPOT OR GAINING EXTRA VACATION TIME. IF YOU WERE GIVEN $1,000,000 AND COULD NOT USE IT TO PAY BILLS, HOW WOULD YOU SPEND IT? HOW DO YOU THINK THIS WOULD CHANGE YOU? IF YOU WERE GIVEN A WEEK OFF, WHAT WOULD YOU DO?

BACKGROUND

We have just observed our differences when it comes to money and time. Today's session will address differences of a more profound nature. Jesus used a parable, a simple story with a deeper meaning, to lead His hearers into new insights about life. We need to keep in mind that a biblical parable is not only intended to teach a principle with a deeper meaning, but also to sort out the mixed motives of its hearers. The parable today will help us see that there are differing responses to the Word of God.

READ

MARK 4:1-20

QUESTIONS FOR INTERACTION:

1. Shoulder to shoulder, thousands of men singing the same songs in one stadium, hearing the same message, yet we all interpret and apply the message differently. How do you explain this?

2. When this farmer sows broadly, where does the seed land?

3. What is the seed in this parable?

PROMISE KEEPERS®
MEN OF INTEGRITY

4 In what ways are the soils a picture of our hearts?

5 Why doesn't the seed germinate equally well in each of the soils?

6 What did Jesus say about the thorns in the soil? What are examples of thorns in our experience?

WRAP-UP. HOW DO WE KNOW WHAT KIND OF SOIL WE ARE? WHAT KIND OF SOIL WOULD YOU LIKE TO BE? WHY?

PROMISE 5: A MAN AND HIS CHURCH

MY RESPONSE AS A PROMISE KEEPER

How can this group help me turn poor soil into good soil? _____

_____

_____

What might be a thorn in my life that is choking the growth of God's Word (seed)? _____

_____

_____

I commit to pray this week for each of these brothers to develop good soil. At our next session, I will ask for a soil report.

WHERE HAVE ALL THE WORRIED FLOWERS GONE?

PROMISE 1: A MAN AND HIS GOD

●●●

WARM-UP. YOU'VE LOST YOUR JOB. IT'S YOUR OWN FAULT. YOUR WIFE IS HAVING AN AFFAIR. YOUR DAUGHTER HAS RUN AWAY FOR THE FOURTH TIME. FINANCIALLY, YOU'VE BLOWN IT. YOUR MATE IS TALKING SEPARATION OR DIVORCE. YOUR PARENT IS AN ALCOHOLIC.

WHAT DOES ANXIETY FEEL LIKE? WHAT IS CREATING ANXIETY IN YOUR LIFE TODAY?

BACKGROUND

In Jesus' Sermon on the Mount, He taught that His Father does not want His children to live anxious lives. Is anxiety-free living really possible?

READ

MATTHEW 6:24–34

QUESTIONS FOR INTERACTION:

1 According to Jesus, what things create anxiety in our lives?

2 What do the birds and the lilies teach us about how to reduce anxiety? How are they involved in meeting their own needs?

3 Why would Jesus say to anxious people, "O men of little faith"?

4 What does it matter that "your heavenly Father knows that you need all these things"?

5 If Jesus doesn't want us to be anxious, what *does* He want us to do? (v. 33)

WRAP-UP: SOMETHING IS WRONG WITH THE CAR. ALAN KNOWS HIS WIFE HAS MOST OF THEIR CHRISTMAS SHOPPING YET TO DO. HE WORRIES THAT THERE IS HARDLY ENOUGH MONEY TO FIX THEIR CAR. IN LIGHT OF THE PRINCIPLES WE'VE STUDIED TODAY, HOW WOULD YOU COUNSEL ALAN?

• •

PROMISE 1: A MAN AND HIS GOD

MY RESPONSE AS A PROMISE KEEPER

In light of the principles we've studied today, how would I counsel *myself* about my own anxiety? _____

_____

_____

_____

_____

THE POWER OF KINDNESS IN A MAN

PROMISE 4: A MAN AND HIS FAMILY

• •

WARM-UP. WHEN JEFF, A BOULDER PROMISE KEEPER, WAS JUST A BOY, HIS GRANDFATHER PROMISED, "SOMEDAY I WILL TAKE YOU TO OUR FAMILY ROOTS IN GERMANY." THIS YOUNG BOY GREW UP WITH THE EXCITEMENT OF SOMEDAY MAKING THAT TRIP. GRANDPA DIDN'T TAKE HIS OWN PROMISES AS SERIOUSLY AS DID HIS GRANDSON, HOWEVER. THE TRIP NEVER HAPPENED.

RECALL A PROMISE MADE TO YOU THAT WAS KEPT OR BROKEN. WHAT HAPPENED? HOW DID YOU FEEL?

BACKGROUND

David had served as Israel's king for about seven years. The highlight of his formative years had been his relationship with Jonathan, son of the former king, Saul. David and Jonathan had made a promise to take care of each others' households should something happen to either of them. Jonathan said to David, "And remember, you must demonstrate the love and kindness of the Lord not only to me during my lifetime, but also to my children after the Lord has destroyed all of your enemies" (1 Sam. 20:15, LB). One day David began wondering if any of Saul's family was still living, for David wanted to be kind to them, just as he had promised.

READ

2 SAMUEL 9:1-13

QUESTIONS FOR INTERACTION:

❶ What might have prompted David's question in verse 1?

❷ How was it that David lost touch with Jonathan's family?

❸ If Mephibosheth's dad and David were Promise Keepers, why was Mephibosheth afraid of David? (What broken promises in his background may have contributed to this fear?)

PROMISE KEEPERS®
MEN OF INTEGRITY

22

4 Why would someone at work or home be afraid to come to you?

5 To what extent did David honor the promise he made to Jonathan?

6 David did not "keep his promises" to his own children, yet he did so with Jonathan's. What might David's children have felt when learning of his care for Mephibosheth?

CONSIDER THIS:

THE MOST WONDERFUL WASTED DAY!

CHARLES FRANCIS ADAMS, A NINETEENTH-CENTURY DIPLOMAT, KEPT A DIARY. ONE DAY HE ENTERED: "WENT FISHING WITH MY SON TODAY – A DAY WASTED." HIS SON, BROOK ADAMS, ALSO KEPT A DIARY. ON THE SAME DAY, BROOK ADAMS MADE THIS ENTRY: "WENT FISHING WITH MY FATHER—MOST WONDERFUL DAY OF MY LIFE."

WRAP-UP: WHY DO MEN TEND TO KEEP PROMISES AT WORK MORE THAN AT HOME? WHO MAY BE THE PERSON AT WORK OR HOME WHO NEEDS MY KIND ATTENTION NOW? (EACH MAN NAME ONE PERSON.)

PROMISE 4: A MAN AND HIS FAMILY

MY RESPONSE AS A PROMISE KEEPER

What specifically can I do to express kindness to the person I named above?

_____

_____

_____

_____

24

THE DEVIL MADE ME DO IT!

PROMISE 3: A MAN AND HIS INTEGRITY

●●●

WARM-UP:

A LOCAL BUSINESSMAN, ASPIRING TO A SEAT ON HIS COMMUNITY'S SCHOOL BOARD, WAS BEING COUNSELED BY THE SUPERINTENDENT: "BILL, IF YOU WILL SOFTEN YOUR STANCE ON ABSTINENCE-BASED SEX EDUCATION, I THINK YOU ARE A SHOO-IN!" HIS LONGTIME DREAM SUDDENLY SEEMS POSSIBLE.

HOW WOULD YOU ADVISE HIM?

BACKGROUND

Many observers would say that Bill will have reached the highest point in his ambitions if he's elected to his school board. Little did he realize he was going to be brought to his lowest point, overcome by the temptation to compromise his convictions. In vivid contrast is the experience of Jesus, who went from the glorious commissioning at His baptism to the depths of the dreadful stalking of the devil in the desert. We can learn much in this session to equip us to face temptation.

READ

MATTHEW 4:1-11

QUESTIONS FOR INTERACTION:

1 What was the first temptation Jesus faced? What was tempting about this for Him?

2 What was the second temptation Jesus faced? What was tempting about this for Him?

3 What was the third temptation Jesus faced? What was tempting about this for Him?

4 Is temptation sin? Why or why not?

5 In his temptation, where did Satan intend to take Jesus ultimately? Where do Satan's temptations try to take us?

6 What did Jesus do in each instance to overcome the devil's allurements?

7 In what ways did the angels of God encourage Jesus?

WRAP-UP:

EACH MAN EXPLAIN HOW HE SEES THIS GROUP ENCOURAGING HIM IN DEALING WITH TEMPTATION. HOW CAN WE PRAY FOR EACH OTHER IN PARTICULAR AREAS OF TEMPTATION (E.G., OVERSPENDING, GREED, FEAR, LUST, REVENGE, PRIDE, ENVY)?

PROMISE 3: A MAN AND HIS INTEGRITY

MY RESPONSE AS A PROMISE KEEPER

I will recognize that the Lord is with me the next time I face the temptation

of _____ .

I will locate a verse of Scripture and memorize it to stand against the temptation (e.g., fear-Ps. 34:4; greed-Mark 8:36; revenge-Rom. 12:19; lust-Ps. 119:9, 11).

"LIKE A GOOD NEIGHBOR"

PROMISE 6: A MAN AND HIS BROTHERS

● ●

WARM-UP: WE LIVE IN COMMUNITIES TODAY WHERE WE HARDLY KNOW OUR NEIGHBORS. OUR WORLD SEEMS IMPERSONAL BECAUSE OF OUR PACE OF LIFE, AND IN A SENSE, WE'RE AFRAID TO GET INVOLVED IN THE LIVES OF PEOPLE.

WHAT QUALITIES DO YOU LOOK FOR IN A GOOD FRIEND OR NEIGHBOR?

BACKGROUND

A neighbor is commonly thought to be the person next door. In the time of the New Testament, however, *neighbor* commonly meant "one living in the same land." Thus, a neighborhood in those days might well have included a number of villages.

READ

LUKE 10:25-37

QUESTIONS FOR INTERACTION:

1 What gives us reason to think this attorney did not love his neighbor? (v. 29)

2 Agree/disagree, and explain your answer: As long as I don't know who my neighbor is, I have no responsibility to him.

3 What did the first two men who encountered this man have in common? Why didn't they stop and help?

4 What motivated the Samaritan to stop and help? What builds compassion in a life?

PK PROMISE
KEEPERS®
MEN OF INTEGRITY

5 If we were traveling the freeway to Jericho, what might keep us from stopping?

6 Under what conditions would you have stopped to help?

7 What does it mean to be a neighbor according to Jesus?

WRAP-UP: IT IS LIKELY, WITHIN A SMALL GROUP LIKE THIS, THAT MEN ARE WOUNDED AND THE GROUP MIGHT UNKNOWINGLY PASS THEM BY. WHAT CAN OUR GROUP DO TO KEEP THIS FROM HAPPENING?

● ●

PROMISE 6: A MAN AND HIS BROTHERS

MY RESPONSE AS A PROMISE KEEPER

What seems to keep me from getting involved in the needs of others, especially those of other cultural backgrounds? _____

_____

_____

_____

I desire to become available to a brother in need this coming week. His name is _____.

POWER TO CHANGE

PROMISE 1: A MAN AND HIS GOD

● ●

WARM-UP. GETTING BETTER AT ANY SPORT USUALLY REQUIRES MORE TIME THAN WE'RE WILLING TO SPEND. THOSE WHO HAVE ACHIEVED EXCELLENCE IN BASKETBALL, FOOTBALL, SOCCER, BOWLING, RACQUETBALL, OR GOLF HAVE DONE SO AT GREAT PERSONAL SACRIFICE. ANY ATHLETE WHO HAS PLAYED A SPORT VERY LONG HAS PICKED UP UNDESIRABLE HABITS, HOWEVER. WHEN HE SEES HIS GAME NEEDING CHANGE, HE SEEKS HELPFUL RESOURCES.

WHAT KINDS OF BAD HABITS DO ATHLETES GET INTO?
WHAT RESOURCES WOULD YOU SUGGEST?

BACKGROUND

When it comes to change in our lives, no one can do a more thorough job than God Himself. A case in point is the apostle Peter, one of God's great trophies. The changes in him were measurable and lasting.

READ

JOHN 13:36–38; 18:15-27

QUESTIONS FOR INTERACTION:

1 Why was Peter so confident that he would not deny his Lord? Why did he fail so miserably?

2 What kinds of things do so many guys want to change in their lives but without much success?

ACTS 4:1–14

3 What was different now about Peter?

"YOU CHRISTIANS SHOULD DWELL ON ONE THING— JESUS CHRIST CHANGES LIVES. IN EVERY STUDENT IN MY CLASS WHO HAS BECOME A CHRISTIAN, AND WHOM I HAVE OBSERVED, I HAVE SEEN A CHANGED LIFE."

4 What explains this change?

UNIVERSITY PHILOSOPHY PROFESSOR

5 You may know someone whose life has been dramatically changed by the Spirit of God. How have most observers attempted to explain the changes?

WRAP-UP. EVERY GOLFER'S DREAM IS TO PLAY A ROUND WITH A PRO LIKE JACK NICKLAUS. BETTER YET, WHAT IF "THE GOLDEN BEAR" WERE TO CLIMB INSIDE YOU AND ACTUALLY PLAY HIS GAME THROUGH YOU? EVERY ASPECT OF YOUR GAME WOULD BE POWERFULLY CHANGED! ALTHOUGH THAT'S NOT REALITY, IT IS TRUE THAT GOD'S SPIRIT LIVES IN YOU AND DESIRES TO LIVE THE LIFE OF JESUS THROUGH YOU. EACH MAN ANSWER: IF THE HOLY SPIRIT WERE TO EMPOWER YOUR LIFE, WHAT CHANGES COULD YOU EXPECT FROM HIM?

ALSO, WHERE IS OUR GROUP ON THE RELATIONAL DIAMOND DESCRIBED ON PAGES 11–12? HOW CAN WE KEEP MOVING AHEAD IN OUR FRIENDSHIPS?

PROMISE 1: A MAN AND HIS GOD

MY RESPONSE AS A PROMISE KEEPER

What one thing would I like God to change today? _____

_____

LET THE WALLS FALL DOWN

● ●

WARM-UP.

RALPH AND TOM ARE ASSOCIATES IN A REALTY FIRM AND HAPPEN TO ATTEND THE SAME CHURCH. RALPH IS ABOUT TO CLOSE ON A DEAL WITH A MUTUAL FRIEND. TOM LEARNS OF THIS IN THE OFFICE AND PRIVATELY GOES TO THEIR MUTUAL FRIEND WITH AN OFFER TO DO THE DEAL FOR HALF THE COMMISSION. THE CLIENT, EAGER TO SAVE MONEY, GOES WITH TOM. WHEN RALPH HEARS OF THIS, HE IS INCENSED.

HOW WOULD YOU GUIDE THESE TWO "BROTHERS" TOWARD RECONCILIATION?

Before reading passage → *I would recommend that they talk to each other to find out why this happened - were there good reasons why Tom did this or was it just to get the deal - maybe he knew the family was in financial trouble, etc.*

BACKGROUND

From time to time in the Christian community, we are going to experience the frustration of being offended or of giving offense to someone. Typically, what we do is brood about it, tell someone else about it, or just do nothing—letting a wall go up between us. Today's paragraph for study gives us the Lord's plan to follow when offenses occur.

READ

MATTHEW 18:15–20

QUESTIONS FOR INTERACTION:

1 What's the first step to take when a fellow Christian sins against us?

discuss it with them first, just the affected parties and try to peacefully resolve it.

2 What two possible responses might he make to our confrontation?

① he could listen, discuss it and work out a peaceful resolution

② get defensive & confrontational

3 What's the next step to take if the fellow Christian is unresponsive?

bring in outside help, a few unaffected people but people knowledgable on the entire situation. In this example a manager or friend in another office would be better than ...

4 The sinning brother adamantly refuses to listen. Now what are we to do?

Probably go to a Church leader to get past the actual sin and find a way to maintain a christian based relationship.

PK PROMISE KEEPERS®
MEN OF INTEGRITY

5 Why go to the church leaders with the matter? And what if he still resists the charges?

(A) Since both people involved are christians in this example: look to a church leader to help determine what how gods word would guide them and ask: What Would Jesus Do?

6 When should we call our local Christian *(B) ?* attorney? (v. 17)

If there is just no peaceful resolution to the conflict and if it really escalates to a legal matter.

7 How authoritative is this process (vv. 15-17) of seeking to resolve a sin between Christians?

not sure I understand the question

8 Where is Jesus in this painful resolution process?

Hopefully, working in the minds and hearts of the people in conflict. To open their hearts and minds to gods words and his teachings to help peacefully resolve the disagreement and to help guide the resolution process as he has taught and in the

WRAP-UP: **WHAT ARE SOME EXAMPLES OF SINS BETWEEN FELLOW CHRISTIANS?** *stages* **WHAT BLOCKS US FROM FOLLOWING JESUS' PLAN FOR MENDING** *depicted* **RELATIONSHIPS? WHY SHOULD WE BOTHER AT ALL TO RESOLVE AN** *in the* **OFFENSE?** *passage*

seemingly immaterial church arguments

we are forgetful and sometimes react as sinful humans instead of taking time to reflect on gods word and **PROMISE 6: A MAN AND HIS BROTHERS** *what Jesus would have us do.*

→ if we don't try to resolve offenses it will just eat away

of someone and build that wall between 2 or more christian brothers

What situation do I need to resolve or reconcile using the principles of today's study? (It may be something that took place years ago?) _____

_____

_____

What brother do I know who needs to resolve a matter with another brother?

_____

How can I encourage this reconciliation? _____

_____

_____

HOW TO BEHAVE IN BAGHDAD

● ●

WARM-UP: YOUR EMPLOYER IS SO IMPRESSED WITH YOUR PERFORMANCE, YOUR ATTITUDE, AND YOUR WORK RELATIONSHIPS THAT HE PULLS YOU ASIDE AND ASKS, "DAVE, WHAT MAKES YOU TICK?" HOW WOULD YOU EXPLAIN WHAT MAKES YOU DIFFERENT?

BACKGROUND

Four young Hebrew men were uprooted from their families in Jerusalem and dumped in Babylon. That's a lot like getting a job transfer from Boulder to Baghdad. Identity, diet, and even values were subject to complete overhaul in these young men's new world. How were they to conduct themselves under these new constraints? As Disraeli, former British prime minister, stated, "Circumstances are beyond the control of man, but his conduct is in his own power." Moving from one workplace to another may never be as dramatic as the story we are about to read, but we can learn from the way these men conducted themselves.

READ

DANIEL 1:1–21

QUESTIONS FOR INTERACTION:

1 Why do you think the God of Israel would place these four choice young men into the kingdom of Nebuchadnezzar?

2 What were the qualifications for serving in Nebuchadnezzar's court?

3 What changes were Daniel and his friends forced to make in this new work environment?

4 What values were being tested in these young men?

5 What was Daniel's critical first step in the process of dealing with his new "employer"? (v. 8)

6 What benefits to "employer" and "employee" are seen in Daniel's creative alternative? (v. 10-16)

7 In what ways did God honor Daniel and his friends when they did what was right?

WRAP-UP: FOR WHAT REASONS MIGHT THE LORD HAVE PLACED YOU "INTO THE HAND" OF YOUR EMPLOYER? SEVERAL MEN GIVE AN ILLUSTRATION OF A DECISION THEY MADE IN THEIR WORKPLACE THAT GOD HAS HONORED.

• •

PROMISE 3: A MAN AND HIS INTEGRITY

MY RESPONSE AS A PROMISE KEEPER

What values have I had tested in my workplace? _____

_____

_____

I, _____ , need to "make up my mind" to _____
       (your name)

_____

_____

_____ .

33

SLEEPLESS IN BAGHDAD

PROMISE 2: A MAN AND HIS FRIENDS

● ●

WARM-UP. A COUPLE OF HOURS INTO A FOUR-HOUR VAN RIDE HOME FROM THE INDIANAPOLIS PROMISE KEEPERS CONFERENCE, CARL DID WHAT MOST OF US FIND DIFFICULT: HE ASKED FOR HELP. "GUYS, I'M IN AN IMPOSSIBLE SITUATION AT WORK, AND I DON'T KNOW WHAT TO DO. I'VE BEEN ASKED TO ALTER THE FIGURES ON EQUIPMENT LEASING IN OUR PROPOSED ANNUAL BUDGET IN ORDER TO GIVE A GOOD REPORT. TOMORROW, I GIVE MY REPORT TO MY MANAGER."

WHAT CAN A VAN FULL OF PROMISE KEEPERS DO TO HELP A GUY LIKE CARL?

BACKGROUND

In chapter 1, Daniel and his three friends were promoted to the king's personal service. Daniel also graduated Phi Beta Kappa in "Dreamology," which now will be tested in the face of Nebuchadnezzar's troubling dream.

READ

DANIEL 2:1-19A

QUESTIONS FOR INTERACTION:

1 What major issue was shaking the king and the kingdom in Babylon (modern-day Baghdad)?

2 How did the king's issue become an impossible situation for his counselors?

3 Contrast the responses of the king's counselors with Daniel's response in this drama. (vv. 10-16)

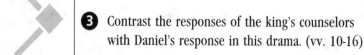

4 In the marketplace, men tend to deal with crises alone. What was Daniel's approach in searching for a solution? (vv. 17-19)

THE PERSON VOTED MVP OF THE NBA EACH YEAR IS NOT ALWAYS THE BEST PLAYER. THERE IS A DIFFERENCE BETWEEN MOST OUTSTANDING AND MOST VALUABLE. THE MVP NOT ONLY TAKES INTO CONSIDERATION SUPERB INDIVIDUAL PERFORMANCE, BUT ALSO THE ABILITY TO INSPIRE AND INVOLVE HIS TEAMMATES, ENCOURAGING AND ENABLING THEM TO EXCEL.

5 Fast forwarding to verse 28, what gave Daniel confidence in his response to the king's impossible request?

6 With a quick look to the end of the chapter, what benefits came to Daniel and his friends for handling their situation the way they did? (vv. 46-49)

WRAP-UP: EACH MAN ANSWER THE FOLLOWING: WHAT FRIENDS, IF ANY, HAVE SUPPORTED YOU IN PAST TIMES OF DISTRESS? WHAT KIND OF SUPPORT DID THEY GIVE (E.G., BEING THERE, MONEY, GIFTS, ADVICE)?

• •

PROMISE 2: A MAN AND HIS FRIENDS

MY RESPONSE AS A PROMISE KEEPER

In light of Daniel's example, what can I do differently the next time I face a crisis? _____

_____

_____

_____

ANOTHER BAD DREAM IN BAGHDAD

PROMISE 1: A MAN AND HIS GOD

- -

WARM-UP: A DYNASTY THEY PREDICTED: TWO SUPER BOWL TROPHIES IN THE COWBOYS' SHOWCASE. "ONE MORE AND WE'RE A DYNASTY!" ON JANUARY 15, 1995, HOWEVER, THE INVINCIBLE DALLAS COWBOYS, ALONG WITH THEIR PRIDE, WERE POUNDED INTO THE TURF OF CANDLESTICK PARK.

WHO COMES TO MIND WHEN YOU THINK OF "PRIDE COMES BEFORE A FALL"? WHY?

BACKGROUND

The story opens with Nebuchadnezzar's praise to the Most High God. This is an incredible conversion account. However, what brought this great king to the point of bowing to God? It was another dream. In this new dream-become-nightmare, the king had to face the future of a man filled with himself. At the heart of this story (and everyone's story, really) is the powerful issue of pride.

READ

DANIEL 4:1-9, 24-37

QUESTIONS FOR INTERACTION:

1 What issue is again troubling the king? (v. 4-7)

2 According to Daniel's interpretations, what was the meaning of the king's nightmare? (vv. 24-26)

3 As horrifying as the nightmare was for the king, there appears to be an "escape clause" (vv. 27-29). How can we explain this?

4 In verse 30, what did Nebuchadnezzar do as a result of God's warning? Why?

5 When did the judgment fall on the king? (vv. 30-31) Why was the judgment so severe?

6 Looking back to when you were a non-Christian, how did God get your attention?

7 How did God bring good out of Nebuchadnezzar's nightmare?

WRAP UP: WHY DOES GOD WORK SO HARD TO ROOT OUT PRIDE? EACH MAN TELL WHO AMONG HIS ACQUAINTANCES MIGHT WELL BE THE OBJECT OF GOD'S ATTENTION-GETTING PROCESS RIGHT NOW. (NO NAMES, PLEASE.)

• •

PROMISE 1: A MAN AND HIS GOD

MY RESPONSE AS A PROMISE KEEPER

What are possible areas of dangerous pride in my life (e.g., my business success, family, reputation)?_____

_____

_____

_____

DANIEL IN THE CRITICS' DEN

● ●

WARM-UP: PEOPLE SEEKING PUBLIC OFFICE OFTEN PEEK THROUGH THE DRAWN CURTAINS TO MAKE SURE THE REPORTERS ARE NOT STAKING OUT THEIR PRIVATE LIVES. WHY IS THERE A NATURAL SUSPICION TOWARD THOSE IN THE PUBLIC SECTOR? SOMETIMES THE FAITH OF A PUBLIC PERSON IS ALSO UNDER SCRUTINY. WHY?

BACKGROUND

At the age of 80, Daniel experienced a distinguished career of public service. Even though he was in the high favor of King Darius, his colleagues felt nothing but hostility toward him. In our culture, the words *character* and *integrity* are mentioned but rarely defined. But rich definition is given to these terms in one of the most well-known stories in all the Bible.

READ

DANIEL 6:1-28

QUESTIONS FOR INTERACTION:

1 What did Daniel's colleagues know to be true about his character?

2 Why did they have a problem with him?

3 Why did they attack his religious beliefs?

4 How did Daniel respond to the king's edict?

PK PROMISE
KEEPERS®
MEN OF INTEGRITY

5 What had Darius observed over time that gave him hope for Daniel's deliverance from the lions?

6 What was ultimately accomplished in the kingdom by the lions' missing a meal that evening?

"DON'T BE LIKE THE CHAMELEON WHO FITS INTO EVERY SITUATION. WHEN HE'S WITH THE PEOPLE IN THE CHURCH, HE'S CHURCHLIKE. BUT WHEN HE'S WITH THE GUYS IN THE STREET, HE'S LIKE ONE OF THE GUYS IN THE STREET. COME OUT FROM AMONG THEM. SHOW THEM THE CONTRADICTION; SHOW THEM THE ALTERNA-TIVE; SHOW THEM HOW A PROMISE KEEPER LIVES!"

BILL MCCARTNEY
FORMER UNIV. OF COLORADO
HEAD FOOTBALL COACH
BOULDER PROMISE KEEPERS
MEN'S CONFERENCE

WRAP-UP. **WHY IS THERE SO OFTEN RESISTANCE TO MEN OF INTEGRITY?**

● ●

PROMISE 3: A MAN AND HIS INTEGRITY

MY RESPONSE AS A PROMISE KEEPER

What qualities in Daniel's life would I like to have in my own? Why? _____

_____

_____

_____

_____

_____

_____

_____

SWIMSUIT EDITION

● ●

WARM-UP: THE ATLANTA AIRPORT IS A LONG WAY FROM JACK'S HOME OR ANYONE HE KNOWS. SPORTS ILLUSTRATED'S NEW SWIMSUIT EDITION HAS JUST HIT THE NEWSSTAND, AND IT CATCHES HIS EYE AS HE WALKS TOWARD GATE A-13. STANDING IN FRONT OF THE NEWSPAPERS, HIS EYES ARE REALLY ON THE SPECIAL S.I. EDITION. WITHIN MINUTES, JACK IS SITTING IN A VACANT GATE AREA WITH A NEW MAGAZINE AND A FRESH APPRECIATION FOR THE LATEST SWIMSUITS. HOW COULD JACK HAVE RESISTED THAT TEMPTATION?

BACKGROUND

The universal appeal of the Psalms for their comfort, wisdom, and insight into the ways of the Lord is readily felt in this gateway selection for today's study. The two paths of life—the way of the godly and the way of the sinful—are clearly in view. Likely we think we're on the first pathway. But do we really know what are its regimens and benefits? Likewise, the consequences of the way of the sinful are often underestimated.

READ

PSALM 1

QUESTIONS FOR INTERACTION:

❶ What is the downward progression of verse 1? How do we see this pattern in today's warm-up?

❷ How do we get the desire to "delight in the law of the Lord"?

❸ What do you think the psalmist had in mind when he said, "And in His law he meditates day and night"?

4 What are the results when we delight in and meditate on the Word? (v.3)

5 What if we don't?

6 What comfort do you find in verse 6?

WRAP-UP. DESCRIBE ONE PERSON YOU KNOW WHO HAS TRAVELED THE DOWNWARD PATH AND ANOTHER WHO CHOSE THE UPWARD PATH. EACH MAN NAME ONE HABIT HE CAN DEVELOP TO PROTECT HIMSELF FROM THE DOWNWARD PATH.

PROMISE 1: A MAN AND HIS GOD

MY RESPONSE AS A PROMISE KEEPER

How can I get the Word of God to be more attractive to me than *Sports Illustrated's* swimsuit edition? _____

_____

_____

_____

THE STATE OF THE UNION

● ●

WARM-UP: ROCKY MOUNTAIN SKI AREAS ARE KNOWN WORLD WIDE FOR THEIR AWESOME SLOPES AND PREMIER POWDER. HOWEVER, A SKIER CANNOT GO JUST ANYWHERE. BOUNDARIES ARE DRAWN TO PROTECT HIM FROM AVALANCHE DISASTER. NONETHELESS, EVERY SEASON FINDS SOMEONE WHO DEFIES THE WARNINGS AND IS DRAWN OUT OF BOUNDS BY THE LURE OF UNSKIED TERRAIN.

KNOWING THE RISK, WHY WOULD A PERSON INTENTIONALLY SKI OUT OF BOUNDS? HOW WOULD YOU REASON WITH HIM IF YOU WERE ASKED TO GO ALONG?

BACKGROUND

In a previous session, we studied the two ways of life: the way of the godly and the way of the sinful. Psalm 1 sets the course of the entire book and is addressed to all people. Psalm 2 is addressed to the leaders of the nations. They, too, must consider the way of the godly and the way of the sinful. A high national price has to be paid when this counsel is ignored.

READ

PSALM 2

QUESTIONS FOR INTERACTION:

1 Why do the kings/national leaders set themselves against the Lord and His Anointed?

2 What does heaven think about all this?

3 What is God's game plan for ultimate world rule?

PROMISE
KEEPERS®
MEN OF INTEGRITY

4 Knowing that the Lord will ultimately rule, how does this affect our perspective on the world today?

5 If you were a congressman or member of Parliament, what would you include in a plan for national blessing?

6 What's happening in our country today that might suggest our leaders are responding to God's warnings?

WRAP-UP. BRAINSTORM THE BENEFITS OF GOD'S BLESSING UPON THOSE WHO "TAKE REFUGE IN HIM."

• •

PROMISE 7: A MAN AND HIS WORLD

MY RESPONSE AS A PROMISE KEEPER

I will rest within the refuge of my God by allowing Christ to rule in my life at home and work.

I will use Psalm 2 as a guide in praying for national leaders.

UNDER THE CIRCUMSTANCES

PROMISE 1: A MAN AND HIS GOD

● ●

WARM-UP: "A SHIPLOAD OF VIETNAM-BOUND YOUNG SAILORS DESPERATELY NEEDS A CHAPLAIN. WE ALL WALKED UP THE GANGPLANK TOGETHER, BUT I KNEW THAT I WAS RESPONSIBLE FOR WHAT THESE YOUNG MEN WOULD DO WITH THE FEARS AND WORRIES THAT ONLY WAR CAN BRING. I WAS SOUNDLY AWARE THAT MY OWN EMOTIONS NEEDED PROTECTION AS WELL. WE STUDIED THE SCRIPTURES AND PRAYED TOGETHER ON THAT LONG FLOAT ACROSS THE SEAS, AND WE DISCOVERED AN AMAZING CALM. IN FACT, I DO NOT PERSONALLY REMEMBER A SINGLE NIGHT'S REST IN MY ONE-YEAR ASSIGNMENT WHEN MY SLEEP WAS INTERRUPTED BY FEAR." U.S. NAVY CHAPLAIN

HOW DO YOU TEND TO RESPOND TO TRYING CIRCUMSTANCES (E.G., WITH YOUR FINANCES, FAMILY, JOB SECURITY, WORK ASSOCIATES)? WHAT HAVE YOU FOUND TO CALM YOUR FEARS?

BACKGROUND

Sensing that there's a design to the order of the Psalms, today's selection moves us from the sweeping view of life and nations we find in Psalms 1 and 2 to an issue of daily reality. How do we handle the fears, foes, and frustrations that come our way as we try to follow the Lord? David wrestled with this, as we all do. But Psalm 3 is more than a rehearsal of woes. The great king and warrior will model the way we can respond when surrounded by overwhelming circumstances.

READ

PSALM 3

QUESTIONS FOR INTERACTION:

❶ Why was David under his circumstances in this psalm?

❷ What good is a shield when under attack?

❸ Why would the king need his head lifted?

PROMISE
KEEPERS®
MEN OF INTEGRITY

4 People in distress often have trouble sleeping. How could David sleep while surrounded by his adversaries?

5 Once the king's personal fears were quieted, what did he need God to do? (v. 7; see also 2 Chron. 21:3 and Prov. 21:31)

CONSIDER THIS:

DR. HOWARD HENDRICKS TELLS OF GREETING A BROTHER WITH, "HOW ARE YOU?" THE MAN RESPONDED, "WELL, UNDER THE CIRCUMSTANCES..." DR. HENDRICKS WAS QUICK TO ASK, "WHAT ARE YOU DOING UNDER THERE?"

6 Why such contrast between verses 1 and 8?

WRAP-UP: IF SOMEONE UNDER THE CIRCUMSTANCES FEELS HELPLESS, HOPELESS, AND WORTHLESS, HOW WILL THIS PSALM LIFT HIS HEAD? EACH MAN CHOOSE ONE WORD TO DESCRIBE A CIRCUMSTANCE THAT IS PRESENTLY PULLING HIM DOWN.

• •

PROMISE 1: A MAN AND HIS GOD

MY RESPONSE AS A PROMISE KEEPER

In light of this psalm, what are some steps I can take to move out from under my circumstances?_____

_____

_____

THE SAGA OF A PROMISE BREAKER

P R O M I S E   6 :   A   M A N   A N D   H I S   B R O T H E R S

• •

WARM-UP.

To Don, the beginning of this year will be different. He has made resolutions he will keep. His painful memories of last year's overpromising have given him a new intensity to stick with his pledges as never before. Included in his resolutions is a promise to spend more time with his daughter. Unfortunately, when March comes, he hears her remind him, "Dad, when will you be able to get to one of my games? The season ends next week!"

WHY DO YOU THINK DON IS HAVING A HARD TIME KEEPING HIS RESOLUTIONS?

BACKGROUND

Israel's first king, Saul, struggled with keeping his promises to God, and thus he disobeyed Him. Sometimes the consequences of disobedience to God are not realized immediately—maybe not until a generation has passed. However, in this account of Israel's national leader, the consequences are both immediate and severe.

READ

1 SAMUEL 15:1–35

QUESTIONS FOR INTERACTION:

1 What had God asked Saul to do?

2 What did the king actually do?

3 Why do you suppose Saul wrestled with making right decisions?

PROMISE
KEEPERS®
MEN OF INTEGRITY

4 What did Saul learn to be the consequences of his disobedience to God?

5 What could Saul have done to keep himself on the throne?

6 What might we conclude when consequences of our disobedience are delayed?

WRAP-UP. AS A GROUP, DISCUSS WHAT MIGHT BE THE CONSEQUENCES IF WE, AS PROMISE KEEPERS, DISOBEY GOD.

• •

PROMISE 6: A MAN AND HIS BROTHERS

MY RESPONSE AS A PROMISE KEEPER

I will make it a point, beginning today, to think before I promise (e.g., regarding schedule, family, church).

I will seek forgiveness with this person for my disobedience: _____

_____.

A River Runs through You

P R O M I S E 1: A M A N A N D H I S G O D

WARM-UP: SOME OF THE MOST SCENIC SPOTS IN NORTH AMERICA ARE IN OUR NATIONAL PARKS. TAKE A MOMENT AND PICTURE A RUSHING MOUNTAIN STREAM, PERHAPS ONE OF YOUR FAVORITES, AND TALK ABOUT THE FEATURES THAT MAKE THIS RIVER YOUR FAVORITE. NOW, WHAT'S WRONG WITH THIS PICTURE: A STAGNANT POOL WITH THE SUBSCRIPT "THE CHRISTIAN LIFE"?

BACKGROUND

Jesus had anything but stagnant water in mind when He spoke in today's section of Scripture. For hundreds of years, on the last day of the harvest Feast of Tabernacles, the high priest would fill a golden vial with water from the Pool of Siloam, attended with the sound of trumpets and thousands of worshipers. Having walked through the gate of the temple to the altar of sacrifice, he elevated the vial and proclaimed the coming Messiah. At this very moment, Jesus leapt to the platform and proclaimed the words of today's text.

READ

JOHN 7:37-39

QUESTIONS FOR INTERACTION:

1 Why do you suppose Jesus described the Holy Spirit's presence in our lives as a flowing river?

2 Why doesn't everyone benefit from the living water?

3 What creates a thirst in a person for this living water? What made you thirsty enough to come to Jesus and believe?

4 When the river of God's Spirit is flowing from someone, what are the benefits to the people around him? Use terms of a rushing river to describe these benefits.

5 Which, if any, of the following tend to restrict the flow of God's living water (His Spirit) in you: mood, circumstances, personality? How are these able to impede such a mighty river?

WRAP-UP: DRAWING UPON OUR COLLECTIVE EXPERIENCES, WHAT ARE SOME SYMPTOMS OF A CHRISTIAN LIFE BECOMING STAGNANT? HOW WOULD EACH MAN DESCRIBE THE FLOW OF LIVING WATER IN HIS LIFE NOW? STAGNANT? INTERMITTENT? TRICKLE? STEADY FLOW?

PROMISE 1: A MAN AND HIS GOD

MY RESPONSE AS A PROMISE KEEPER

In the coming days, when I see the "flow" being restricted, what will I do?

_____

_____

What would my life look like with "a river running through it"? _____

_____

_____

How would this benefit those around me? _____

_____

_____

RESPONDING TO YOUR WIFE'S CRISIS

P R O M I S E   4 :   A   M A N   A N D   H I S   F A M I L Y

WARM-UP: YOUR WIFE HAS EXTENDED THE FAMILY'S CREDIT BEYOND YOUR ABILITY TO MAKE PAYMENTS BY BUYING NEEDED SCHOOL CLOTHES FOR YOUR KIDS. HOW CAN YOU BE SUPPORTIVE OF HER AND YET PAY THE DEBT?

BACKGROUND

Unlike today's engagement process, engagement in the first century consisted of a legal bond that could only be broken by divorce. Also, the law demanded that an adulteress be divorced—stoning didn't always follow unless the offended made the issue public. Since Mary was pregnant before her wedding, people would have assumed she was guilty of adultery.

READ

MATTHEW 1:18–25

QUESTIONS FOR INTERACTION:

1 How much more difficult was it then than now to explain the dilemma of pregnancy outside of marriage? Why?

2 Why do you think Mary was selected to give birth to the Son of God? What did Joseph have to do with her being selected?

3 Why did God cause Mary to become pregnant during the engagement?

4 Why was Joseph afraid to take Mary as his wife?

5 What motivated Joseph to have compassion in Mary's dilemma?

6 How have you seen other husbands show honor to their wives?

7 What fresh insights do you now have in responding to our warm-up story?

CONSIDER THIS:

TO HOUSTON OILERS' STARTING RIGHT TACKLE DAVID WILLIAMS, BIRTH IS NO TIME FOR PLAYING GAMES. WILLIAMS SKIPPED HIS TEAM'S 28-14 AWAY-GAME WIN OVER THE NEW ENGLAND PATRIOTS AND REMAINED HOME WITH HIS WIFE, WHO HAD JUST GIVEN BIRTH TO THEIR FIRST CHILD. THE OILERS' MANAGEMENT WAS NOT AMUSED AND DOCKED WILLIAM'S PAY $111,000. "I DON'T REGRET WHAT I'VE DONE," SAID WILLIAMS. "MY FAMILY COMES FIRST!"

JOHN W. KENNEDY
CHRISTIANITY TODAY
DECEMBER 13, 1993

WRAP-UP: FOR EACH OF YOU WHO ARE MARRIED, WHAT TWO OR THREE WAYS WOULD YOUR WIFE SAY YOU ESTEEM OR HONOR HER? WHY IS DOING THIS IMPORTANT?

• •

PROMISE 4: A MAN AND HIS FAMILY

MY RESPONSE AS A PROMISE KEEPER

This week I will honor and serve my wife by: _____

_____

_____

_____.

"CALL 911!"

● ●

WARM-UP.

OCTOBER 8, 1994, OPENING DAY OF ELK SEASON. THE SAN JUAN MOUNTAINS NORTH OF DURANGO, COLORADO, WERE RECEIVING RECORD SNOWFALL. KYLE WAS HUNTING IN TWO FEET OF NEW POWDER. VISIBILITY WAS AT ITS WORST. HE HAD FORGOTTEN HIS COMPASS, AND BY 10:00 P.M. HE WAS HOPELESSLY LOST. HIS MIND WAS FLOODED WITH FEARS. KYLE BROKE HIS FRANTIC PACE BY STOPPING UNDER A MASSIVE PONDEROSA PINE. ONLY THEN DID THE TERROR IN HIS HEART SETTLE, PROVIDING NEEDED PERSPECTIVE. IT WAS A LONG AND COLD NIGHT, BUT HE FELT SECURE IN THE SHADOW OF THAT GIANT TREE. WHAT FEARS MIGHT HAVE GRIPPED KYLE THAT NIGHT?

BACKGROUND

Psalm 91 is an incredible testimony to the security of those who trust in God. The author of this psalm is anonymous, but it was probably written by one of the temple personnel (a priest or Levite) as a word of assurance to those who obey and follow God.

READ

PSALM 91

QUESTIONS FOR INTERACTION:

1 If Kyle could have read or recalled Psalm 91, what would have calmed his fears? (vv. 1-4)

2 If we stay in the shadow of the Almighty, what does it do for us? (vv. 5-9)

PROMISE
KEEPERS®
MEN OF INTEGRITY

3 "My teenager is out of control. I think she's contemplating suicide!" What can we say to this dad to help him with perspective?

4 How is the deliverance of God here so different from "The man upstairs is always there" or "May the force be with you"?

WRAP-UP:

THERE'S A NATURAL HESITATION TO CALL "911" WHEN WE'RE NOT SURE OUR CRISIS IS MAJOR ENOUGH. BUT WITH THE LORD, IT IS ALWAYS OKAY TO CALL! WHAT DO EACH OF YOU ANTICIPATE AS A "911" CALL TO GOD THIS WEEK?

ALSO, WHERE IS OUR GROUP NOW ON THE RELATIONAL DIAMOND DESCRIBED ON PAGES 11–12? HOW CAN WE KEEP MOVING AHEAD IN OUR FRIENDSHIPS?

• •

PROMISE 1: A MAN AND HIS GOD

MY RESPONSE AS A PROMISE KEEPER

This week, should sleep evade me, I will call "911." Memorize Psalm 91:1. When Almighty God answers (and He always does), I will praise Him with the words of Psalm 91.

PLANS FOR LUNCH?

● ●

WARM-UP: WHAT IF THIS HEADLINE STORY WERE TO APPEAR IN YOUR CITY'S NEWSPAPER: "JESUS CHRIST VISITS CITY FOR THREE DAYS— LOVED BY MOST, HATED BY A FEW!" WHERE WOULD HE LIKELY SPEND MOST OF HIS TIME? WHO WOULD MOST LIKELY PROTEST HIS VISIT? WHAT WOULD YOU DO TO DEMONSTRATE YOUR INTEREST IN SEEING HIM?

BACKGROUND

Jesus was on His way to Jerusalem, where before long He would be crucified. This adds something to today's story, because the man Jesus met was one of the last men He would call to Himself before He was put to death. On this bright spring morning when Jesus came to town, the man was sitting on the veranda of the imposing house he had built with the profits of extortion.

READ

LUKE 19:1–10

QUESTIONS FOR INTERACTION:

1 Given who Zaccheus was, why would he have any interest in seeing Jesus?

2 Why would Jesus have any interest in Zaccheus?

3 What needs in Zaccheus' life may be common to those successful in the business community?

PK PROMISE
KEEPERS®
MEN OF INTEGRITY

4 Why did Jesus insist on going to Zaccheus' house instead of just talking to him in the tree?

5 What did Jesus see in Zaccheus that was totally missed by the protestors?

6 What evidence is there for radical transformation in Zaccheus? What must have been part of this lunchtime conversation to bring about such radical change?

WRAP-UP: WHAT HAVE YOU LEARNED IN THIS SESSION ABOUT MINISTERING IN YOUR WORKPLACE?

PROMISE 7: A MAN AND HIS WORLD

MY RESPONSE AS A PROMISE KEEPER

What evidence can be seen in my home that "salvation has come to this house" (e.g., unselfishness, honesty, goodwill, kindness)? _____

_____

_____

_____

If my house is not in order, then like Zaccheus, I will invite Jesus to help loosen my grip on my money and my goods, and to help me serve those I may have wronged.

So, What's Wrong with Being Rich?

PROMISE 1: A MAN AND HIS GOD

WARM-UP: MOST OF US THINK WE WOULD BE UNAFFECTED BY LARGE SUMS OF MONEY COMING TO US, WHETHER BY INHERITANCE OR SIMPLY GOOD BUSINESS DECISIONS. WHY DOES MONEY DO FUNNY THINGS TO PEOPLE? SO, WHAT'S WRONG WITH BEING RICH?

BACKGROUND

The story of the rich, young ruler must have made a deep impression on the Gospel writers, for he appears in Matthew, Mark, and Luke. From Matthew we learn of his youth; from Luke we learn that he was among the ruling class of his day. His wealth was also in sharp contrast to the simple lifestyle of the unsophisticated Galileans. This young man probably belonged to a social group unreached by the gospel.

READ

LUKE 18:18-27

QUESTIONS FOR INTERACTION:

1 What makes a successful businessman think he can achieve immortality on his own?

2 The love of money does funny things to people. What did it do to this young ruler that it didn't do to Zaccheus? (Luke 19)

3 Why was Jesus so extreme (18:22) in His approach with this man compared to Zaccheus? (Luke 19:8)

4 The account of this story in Mark mentions that Jesus felt a love for this young man that cushioned His conversation with him. Why must this attitude be at the heart of our Christian witness?

5 Sadly, there are hundreds of modern stories like this one. What gives us hope that such money-controlled people will experience eternal life?

WRAP-UP: WHAT ARE THE SYMPTOMS OF A FAMILY BECOMING ATTACHED TO MONEY?

PROMISE 1: A MAN AND HIS GOD

MY RESPONSE AS A PROMISE KEEPER

What do I own that I can't give away? _____
_____

How do I keep my heart from becoming attached to it? _____
_____
_____

How can I develop a heart of love for money-controlled people? _____
_____
_____

FROM HERE TO ETERNITY

P R O M I S E   3 :   A   M A N   A N D   H I S   I N T E G R I T Y

• •

WARM-UP. MOST OF US ARE RELUCTANT TO GIVE MANY DETAILS CONCERNING OUR FINANCIAL AFFAIRS. THIS MAY BE FOR GOOD REASON, BECAUSE MOST OF US STRUGGLE WITH SIMPLY BALANCING OUR CHECKBOOKS. WHY WOULD A LEADING FINANCIAL COUNSELOR SAY, "A QUICK LOOK INTO A PERSON'S CHECKBOOK TELLS ME MORE ABOUT HIM THAN ANYTHING ELSE"?

BACKGROUND

After Jesus encountered Zaccheus in Jericho, He and His disciples continued their journey toward Jerusalem. By now, these close followers were convinced that Jesus would soon defeat Rome and set up His throne in Jerusalem. To bring them back to the reality of daily stewardship, He explained the parable in today's session.

READ

LUKE 19:11–27

QUESTIONS FOR INTERACTION:

❶ What did the nobleman ask of his subjects?

❷ Why do you think most of his citizens responded with a rebellious spirit?

❸ Not everybody rebelled; some responded positively. What did they do?

PROMISE
KEEPERS®
MEN OF INTEGRITY

4 What benefits came to the two good servants?

5 What do you think is the point of the parable?

.

6 In what sense is the severe ending of this story applicable to us today? (Surely each of us has either personally gone through or knows others who have experienced the devastating result of financial mismanagement.)

WRAP-UP: WHY ARE PERSONAL FINANCES MORE DIFFICULT TO TALK ABOUT THAN MOST OTHER PERSONAL MANAGEMENT ISSUES?

● ●

PROMISE 3: A MAN AND HIS INTEGRITY

MY RESPONSE AS A PROMISE KEEPER

If someone were to assess my personal checkbook, what might he discover (e.g., integrity, giving back to God, greed)? _____

_____

_____

If money management is a real need in my life, what steps might I take to get started (e.g., seek counsel from a friend with expertise, check the church library for resources)? _____

_____

My financial stewardship is important to God. This week I will pause for prayer before any decision involving money.

HEARTBREAK HOTEL

PROMISE 4: A MAN AND HIS FAMILY

••

WARM-UP. CINDY HAD BEEN LOOKING FORWARD TO AN ESCAPE WEEKEND WITH HER HUSBAND, DAVE, FOR SOME TIME. THEIR HOTEL ROOM WAS DECORATED JUST AS SHE WOULD HAVE DONE IT. DAVE DOESN'T HAVE ESPN AT HOME, SO HE WAS THRILLED TO BE THERE AS WELL. "WHAT A GREAT, UNHURRIED TIME FOR THE TWO OF US TO TALK OVER PLANS FOR A FAMILY," CINDY MENTIONED TO DAVE, WHO WAS DEEPLY INVOLVED IN WATCHING A GAME. THE FOLLOWING DAY OVER LUNCH, HER TEARING EYES SENT A MESSAGE OF DISAPPOINTMENT TO DAVE. WHY WAS SHE CRYING? WHAT SHOULD DAVE DO ABOUT IT?

BACKGROUND

A great prophet, Samuel was a man mightily used by God in anointing Israel's first king and then David, his successor. What we may not know is the wonderful beginning to Samuel's life. First Samuel opens with the amazing story of his mother, Hannah. She found herself in a seemingly hopeless situation, going through all the emotions associated with such distress. But her actions told of her true character and heart.

READ

1 SAMUEL 1:1–11

QUESTIONS FOR INTERACTION:

1 What was the root of Hannah's sorrow?

2 What barriers to a happy marriage did she face?

3 A vow is not a "letter of intent," but rather a promise to God. Why did Hannah resort to a vow?

1 SAMUEL 1:12–18

"WE GROW AND MATURE SPIRITUALLY THROUGH ADVERSITY—NOT WHEN EVERYTHING IS GOING SMOOTHLY. IN A TIME OF ADVERSITY AND TROUBLE, THE CHRISTIAN HAS THE OPPORTUNITY TO KNOW GOD IN A SPECIAL AND PERSONAL WAY."

4 How did Hannah follow through on her vow?

5 How did Hannah demonstrate her faith in God?

C. EVERETT KOOP
FORMER U.S. SURGEON
GENERAL
LEADERSHIP JOURNAL
FALL 1994

1 SAMUEL 1:19–28

6 Why would following through on this vow be so difficult for Hannah?

7 In today's world, what does it mean to give our children back to God?

WRAP-UP: EACH MAN TELL OF ONE WAY HE HAS COMFORTED HIS WIFE IN A TIME OF NEED.

● ●

PROMISE 4: A MAN AND HIS FAMILY

MY RESPONSE AS A PROMISE KEEPER

If God has entrusted me with children, have I given them back to Him? _____

_____

I will discuss this with my wife and children this week.

HANNAH'S HALLMARK OF PRAYER

PROMISE 1: A MAN AND HIS GOD

●●

WARM-UP: TED HAS BEEN A CHRISTIAN FOR NEARLY 10 YEARS. TALKING WITH GOD USED TO BE SO NATURAL, BUT NOW HE WONDERS IF PRAYING REALLY MATTERS THAT MUCH. OH, HE PRAYS BEFORE MEALS AND OCCASIONALLY WHEN ASKED IN CHURCH, BUT GOD DOESN'T HEAR MUCH FROM TED OTHERWISE. HIS WIFE HAS NOTICED IT AS WELL. WHAT HAS TED'S WIFE LIKELY OBSERVED? HOW WOULD YOU HELP TED IN HIS PRAYER LIFE?

BACKGROUND

Hannah's dramatic answer to prayer for a son rejuvenated her confidence in God. However, there is something strangely wonderful about the recorded prayer of this mother who put God first, kept her vow to Him, and gave Him great praise.

READ

1 SAMUEL 2:1-11

QUESTIONS FOR INTERACTION:

1 What are the usual components of prayer? What was so unusual about Hannah's prayer?

2 In what ways was her prayer more profound than simply one of thanksgiving?

3 List the many ways in which Hannah described God. What does each of them mean?

4 How did Hannah's sufferings and sorrows affect the way she prayed?

5 What have you experienced that has profoundly affected your prayer life?

WRAP-UP. PRAY TOGETHER AS A GROUP—WITHOUT THANKSGIVING, WITHOUT REQUESTS, WITHOUT CONFESSION, BUT ONLY WITH PRAISE.

• •

PROMISE 1: A MAN AND HIS GOD

MY RESPONSE AS A PROMISE KEEPER

Why are my prayers usually unlike Hannah's?_____

_____

_____

_____

This week I will purpose to pray in a new way, like Hannah.

JUST SAY NO!

● ●

WARM-UP. LIVING IN A CULTURE DOMINATED BY SENSUALITY, NEARLY EVERY DAY WE ARE LURED TOWARD IMMORALITY. MOST EVERY NEWSPAPER DAY, WE READ OF ANOTHER PROMINENT AMERICAN LEADER WHO FALLS INTO SEXUAL SIN. WHAT CAUSES SOMEONE TO SELL OUT HIS REPUTATION SO CHEAPLY? HOW HAS THE LIFE OF SOMEONE YOU KNOW BEEN AFFECTED?

BACKGROUND

Joseph was next to the youngest of 12 children. At the age of 17, he was sold into slavery by his own brothers and taken to Egypt. God had a plan for this young man that placed him in a highly responsible position in the palace of Egypt's pharaoh. Joseph was only in his 20s in Genesis 39, but he showed wisdom well beyond his years.

READ

GENESIS 39

QUESTIONS FOR INTERACTION:

❶ Why did Joseph's boss trust him so totally?

❷ What made Joseph so desirable to this man's wife?

❸ Why was Joseph so vulnerable to her sexual advances? What makes us vulnerable?

PROMISE
KEEPERS®
MEN OF INTEGRITY

4 If Joseph were in our group here, how might we have helped him in dealing with the advances of his boss's wife?

5 What were Joseph's reasons for saying no? What enabled him to move from reason to responsible action?

6 What can be the cost of maintaining moral purity? What can be the benefits?

WRAP-UP. WHAT SIGNALS ARE EMITTED BY A PERSON ATTRACTED TO YOU? TALK TOGETHER ABOUT HOW THIS GROUP CAN HELP EACH OTHER SAY NO.

• •

PROMISE 3: A MAN AND HIS INTEGRITY

MY RESPONSE AS A PROMISE KEEPER

What have I learned to do about sexual lust and temptation, since a man rarely outgrows his sexual passions?_____

_____

_____

Joseph is my model of moral purity. When immoral thoughts enter my mind, I will ask the Lord to make me strong like Joseph.

WHEN FAMILIES FORGIVE

P R O M I S E   6 :   A   M A N   A N D   H I S   B R O T H E R S

• •

WARM-UP. TWO BROTHERS TOOK OVER THEIR DAD'S BUSINESS UPON HIS DEATH. WITHIN THE FIRST YEAR THE YOUNGER BROTHER LEGALLY FORCED HIS OLDER BROTHER OUT. THE BITTERNESS OF THIS BREAKUP HAS DESTROYED THE WHOLE FAMILY.

WHAT MUST HAPPEN FOR FAMILY RECONCILIATION TO TAKE PLACE?

BACKGROUND

Joseph had nearly doubled in age since he was sold into slavery by his jealous brothers. Now he had to confront deep-seated hurt as he faced his family. God had kept His hand on Joseph's life and placed him as prime minister, where he saved the country from great famine. In the meantime, his own Jewish family, thinking Joseph was dead, came to Egypt to purchase food. Joseph disguised himself from his brothers, but as we read Genesis 45, Joseph could contain himself no longer. Would he seek revenge or reconciliation, give a curse or a blessing?

READ

GENESIS 45

QUESTIONS FOR INTERACTION:

1 What emotions overwhelmed Joseph when he met with his brothers?

2 What emotions were his brothers likely feeling at that same moment? What emotions of unforgiveness (pain, revenge, anger, humiliation, self-pity) have you experienced within your family?

3 What kind of emotional suffering do you suppose Joseph experienced over the years since his brothers abandoned him?

PROMISE
K E E P E R S®
MEN OF INTEGRITY

4 How was Joseph able to be so forgiving of his brothers?

5 How does Joseph teach us that forgiveness is more than words?

6 What were the benefits of forgiveness in Joseph's life? What were the benefits of forgiveness in Joseph's family?

WRAP-UP. WHY IS GRANTING FORGIVENESS WITHIN ONE'S FAMILY SELDOM EASY? EACH MAN TELL WHO IN HIS FAMILY MIGHT NEED HIS FORGIVENESS.

• •

PROMISE 6: A MAN AND HIS BROTHERS

MY RESPONSE AS A PROMISE KEEPER

What brothers-in-Christ from different ethnic and cultural backgrounds need my forgiveness?_____

_____

What would keep me from offering forgiveness? _____

_____

Benefits to my reconciled family and to me will be _____

_____

_____.

The benefits to my reconciled brothers and to me will be _____

_____

_____.

DECIDE TO ABIDE

● ●

WARM-UP. OLD JED AND HIS CRONIES PIONEERED THEIR WAY INTO NORTHERN ALASKA TO FIND THEIR GOLDEN FUTURE. THEIR CAMP, ON A WELL-TRAVELED SUPPLY ROUTE, TOOK ON A FEEL OF HOME, WHILE GOLD PRODUCTION WAS QUITE PROFITABLE. TO THE SURPRISE OF HIS FRIENDS, ONE DAY JED DECIDED TO HEAD DEEP INTO THE BROOKS RANGE AND LIVE ON HIS OWN.

WHY WOULD JED SEPARATE HIMSELF? WHAT WILL JED MISS BY LEAVING HIS CRONIES?

| BACKGROUND | READ |

Jesus and His close friends had just completed the last supper. Along their way to Gethsemane, they passed through a vineyard. Here Jesus described the vital link between Himself and His close friends.

JOHN 15:1-11

QUESTIONS FOR INTERACTION:

1 What is the connection between the vine and its branches?

2 What is the key to maximum fruit-bearing?

3 Why does a vinedresser prune his valued fruit? Why does God prune His people? What does pruning include?

4 What do we receive from Christ as a result of His life flowing through us (i.e., abiding)?

5 People do things all the time without Christ. Why would He say, "For apart from Me you can do nothing"?

6 How difficult is it for a branch to abide in its vine? How do we abide in Christ?

WRAP-UP. **WHAT IS TRUE OF THIS GROUP SINCE EACH OF US IS A BRANCH OF THE VINE?**

• •

PROMISE 2: A MAN AND HIS FRIENDS

MY RESPONSE AS A PROMISE KEEPER

I will write "I am in the Vine" on one side of a 3x5 card.

I will use the other side of the card to draw a vine with its branches, label-ing the branches with my brothers' names from this group.

I will use this card every day when I pray.

"SO, WHAT'S THE BIG DEAL ABOUT THE CHURCH?"

P R O M I S E   5 :   A   M A N   A N D   H I S   C H U R C H

WARM-UP. IN OUR HIGH-TECH SOCIETY, THE CHURCH CAN BE DISMISSED AS A RELIC OF THE PAST—OF NO SIGNIFICANCE. IT IS SEEN AS NECESSARY ONLY FOR A WEDDING SITE, A PLACE TO DROP OFF THE KIDS ON SUNDAY MORNING, OR FOR MAKING A FEW BUSINESS CONTACTS.

WHY DOES THE WORLD FAIL TO SEE THE CHURCH FOR WHAT IT REALLY IS? WHAT DO YOU THINK IS THE REPUTATION OF YOUR CHURCH IN YOUR COMMUNITY?

BACKGROUND

Our Lord said in Matthew's Gospel, "I will build My church; and the gates of hell will not prevail against it." This suggests that the church is God's personal project and that it will be perpetually invincible. With all its quirks and weaknesses, it still stands head and shoulders above all other institutions. Recognizing its timeless importance, the author of Hebrews calls us to fresh appreciation of the church's strategic place in our lives—centering us in God's plan.

READ

HEBREWS 10:19–25

QUESTIONS FOR INTERACTION:

1 Why do we enthrone Jesus as Head of the church?

2 What are some of the benefits of meeting together as a church? (vv. 23-25)

3 Why do a lot of Christians become negligent in their church life?

PROMISE
KEEPERS®
MEN OF INTEGRITY

4 What perspective does the church give us that we can get nowhere else?

5 What issues of life is the church uniquely gifted to handle?

6 What can the church provide in the midst of our secular and godless culture?

CONSIDER THIS:

PERCENTAGE OF AMERICANS WHO BELIEVE THE CHURCH HAS INFLUENCED SOCIETY IN A POSITIVE WAY: 85

PERCENTAGE WHO BELIEVE COMPUTERS AND TECH-NOLOGY HAVE: 87

LEADERSHIP JOURNAL
SPRING 1993

WRAP-UP. WHAT HAS BEEN THE CHURCH'S IMPACT ON SOCIETY (E.G., SCHOOLS, HOSPITALS)? EACH MAN DESCRIBE THE CHURCH'S IMPACT ON HIM.

• •

PROMISE 5: A MAN AND HIS CHURCH

MY RESPONSE AS A PROMISE KEEPER

Since I see the church in a fresh light, I will _____

_____

_____ .

I will encourage my pastor this week by _____

_____

_____ .

BENT ON MENTORING

• •

WARM-UP. JIM IS AN ELECTRICAL CONTRACTOR, IN BUSINESS FOR HIMSELF. AS A JOURNEYMAN ELECTRICIAN, HE OFTEN CONTEMPLATES WHO COULD TAKE OVER FOR HIM AND WHO COULD WORK ALONGSIDE HIM NOW AS AN APPRENTICE. WHY MIGHT JIM WANT TO FIND AN APPRENTICE? WHAT DOES A JOURNEYMAN LIKE JIM LOOK FOR IN AN APPRENTICE? HOW LONG DO YOU SUPPOSE IT TAKES TO MOVE FROM APPRENTICE TO JOURNEYMAN?

BACKGROUND

The terms *journeyman, mentor, junior partner, senior partner, rookie, veteran, apprentice,* and *trainee* reflect the process necessary for becoming a professional expert. The apostle Paul understood the need to pass on what he had learned about life to his son in the faith, Timothy.

READ

2 TIMOTHY 2:1–10

QUESTIONS FOR INTERACTION:

1 Why would Paul's first concern for Timothy be that he "be strong in the grace that is in Christ Jesus"?

2 The journeyman has a plan for the apprentice. What was Paul's plan for his apprentice?

3 What does *soldier* tell us about the dedication required of an apprentice? What does *athlete* tell us about the discipline required? What does *farmer* tell us about the diligence needed?

4 What confidence did Paul have that Timothy would grasp the plan?

5 Why must we have spiritual mentors? What happens if we don't?

WRAP-UP:

WHAT QUALIFIES SOMEONE TO BE A SPIRITUAL MENTOR? WHOM MIGHT GOD BE GIVING TO EACH OF US AS A "TIMOTHY" (E.G., DAUGHTER, SON, SON-IN-LAW, WORK ASSOCIATE)?

WHERE IS OUR GROUP NOW ON THE RELATIONAL DIAMOND DESCRIBED ON PAGES 11–12? HOW CAN WE KEEP MOVING AHEAD IN OUR FRIENDSHIPS?

PAGES 11–12?

· ·

PROMISE 2: A MAN AND HIS FRIENDS

MY RESPONSE AS A PROMISE KEEPER

What are the implications for my life if I refuse the person seeking to be mentored by me? _____

_____

What are the implications for the life of a "Timothy" being refused? _____

_____

_____

BENT BY MENTORING

● ●

WARM-UP: TOM KNEW HE WAS JUST AN AVERAGE HIGH-SCHOOL QUARTERBACK, NEVER STARTING BUT GETTING SOME PLAYING TIME. BUT IN THE OFF-SEASON OF HIS JUNIOR YEAR, HE DISCOVERED THAT A FORMER ALL-PRO QUARTERBACK HAD MOVED IN DOWN THE STREET. OVER THE SUMMER MONTHS, TOM ACQUIRED SKILLS HE NEVER DREAMT POSSIBLE THROUGH THE COACHING OF THIS NEW ACQUAINTANCE. WHAT IF TOM HAD NEVER DISCOVERED THIS PERSON?

NAME SOMEONE WHO HAS INFLUENCED YOU, AND HOW. WHAT IF YOU HAD NEVER DISCOVERED THIS PERSON?

BACKGROUND

He was a young believer. His mother was Jewish, his father a Greek. Most of his spiritual development came from the influence of Eunice, his mother, and Lois, his grandmother. Not until Timothy began to follow the apostle Paul did he gain the skills to provide leadership for a church.

READ

1 TIMOTHY 4:12-16

QUESTIONS FOR INTERACTION:

1 Why is there a natural tendency to look down on youthfulness?

2 How did Paul suggest that Timothy overcome the criticisms of his elders concerning his youthfulness?

3 Why is age not a criterion for spiritual leadership?

4 What qualities does an apprentice demonstrate to attract someone to mentor him?

5 What part did spiritual giftedness play in the life of Timothy?

6 What benefits come to our lives when we seek to be mentored? What benefits come to the life of a mentor when an apprentice seeks his leadership?

WRAP-UP. WHY DO SO FEW CHRISTIAN MEN TAKE THE INITIATIVE TO FIND A MENTOR? WHOM MIGHT GOD BE GIVING TO EACH OF US AS A "PAUL" (E.G., A WORK ASSOCIATE, FATHER-IN-LAW, GOOD FRIEND, PASTOR, FELLOW CHURCHMAN)?

● ●

PROMISE 2: A MAN AND HIS FRIENDS

MY RESPONSE AS A PROMISE KEEPER

What are the implications for my life if I refuse to seek a mentor?_____

_____

_____

What are the implications for a "Paul" if I refuse his mentoring? _____

_____

_____

THE WIND BENEATH MY WINGS

PROMISE 5: A MAN AND HIS CHURCH

• •

WARM-UP: WINNING A HEISMAN TROPHY IS NOT SOMETHING YOU DO ALONE, AND
THE 1994 WINNER, RASHAAN SALAAM, WAS THE FIRST TO ACKNOWL-
EDGE THOSE WHO ENCOURAGED HIM AS HE WAS ELEVATED TO THE TOP.
HIS COACH, COLORADO UNIVERSITY'S BILL MCCARTNEY, KEPT
RASHAAN FROM QUITTING AS AN UNDERCLASSMAN. HIS TEAM'S
OFFENSIVE LINE PROVIDED HIM THE ENCOURAGEMENT TO RUN WITH
ABANDON. AND "MY MOTHER, KHALADA, HAS BEEN THE MOST INFLU-
ENTIAL PERSON IN MY LIFE," HE ADDED.

THROUGH DIFFERENT STAGES OF YOUR LIFE, WHO HAS ENCOURAGED
YOU THE MOST, AND HOW?

BACKGROUND

Saul of Tarsus was the
original Christian killer.
His reputation for hating
Christians preceded him
wherever he traveled.
Naturally, those who
followed Jesus in those
days were leery when
Saul expressed an interest
in following Christ.
However, one young man
was neither afraid nor
intimidated by Saul's reputation. Barnabas was used
by God to come along-
side this feared man on a
number of occasions that
changed history.

READ

ACTS 4:34–37

QUESTIONS FOR INTERACTION:

1 Why do you suppose the apostles renamed
Joseph?

2 What did Barnabas do that was encouraging?

READ

ACTS 9:26–29

3 Why didn't the Christians in Jerusalem believe
Saul had been converted?

PK PROMISE KEEPERS®
MEN OF INTEGRITY

76

4 What did Barnabas do that was encouraging?

READ

ACTS 15:36–41

5 What was the dispute between Paul and Barnabas?

6 What did Barnabas do that was encouraging?

CONSIDER THIS:

"FRIENDS IN YOUR LIFE ARE LIKE PILLOWS ON YOUR PORCH. SOMETIMES THEY HOLD YOU UP, AND SOMETIMES THEY LEAN ON YOU. SOMETIMES IT'S JUST ENOUGH TO KNOW THEY'RE STANDING BY."

ANONYMOUS

WRAP-UP. WHOM HAS GOD GIVEN TO EACH OF US AS "WIND BENEATH OUR WINGS," A "BARNABAS" IN OUR LIVES (E.G., WIFE, WORK ASSOCIATE, PASTOR, PARENT)?

• •

PROMISE 5: A MAN AND HIS CHURCH

MY RESPONSE AS A PROMISE KEEPER

To whom could I be a "Barnabas" (e.g., family member, work associate, pastor, fellow churchman)? _____

How could I be a "Barnabas" (son of encouragement) to my pastor this week?

_____

_____

You've Gotta Have Heart

P R O M I S E   4 :   A   M A N   A N D   H I S   F A M I L Y

●●

WARM-UP: 1994's NOVEMBER NEWS ANNOUNCED THAT A CERTAIN NEW ENGLAND PASTOR OFFERED FORGIVENESS TO THE MAN WHO KILLED HIS SON. THE PASTOR EVEN HELPED HIM GET OUT OF PRISON. "TODAY, THE REVEREND WALTER EVERETT WILL OFFICIATE AT THE CONNECTICUT WEDDING OF HIS SON'S KILLER!"

WHY WOULD THIS MAN FORGIVE? HOW COULD THIS MAN FORGIVE?

BACKGROUND

READ

Forgiveness is more than a nice idea. It's absolutely critical that we grasp it if God's will is ever to be fulfilled in our lives. Forgiveness is difficult. Often it's illogical. We also can't extend forgiveness unless we have received it.

 MATTHEW 18:21–35

QUESTIONS FOR INTERACTION:

❶ How did Peter view forgiveness?

❷ What did Jesus hope Peter would see regarding forgiveness?

❸ Who might Jesus have had in mind in His story? (vv. 23-27)

❹ As the story continues in 19:28-34, what was the difference in the size of the two debts?

PK PROMISE KEEPERS®
MEN OF INTEGRITY

78

5 Why might the servant who had been forgiven so much have been so severe about the debt owed him?

6 How will the offended brother know he has been forgiven from the heart?

CONSIDER THIS:

"WHEN YOU FORGIVE SOMEONE WHO HURT YOU, YOU ARE DANCING TO THE RHYTHM OF THE DIVINE HEARTBEAT."

DR. LEWIS B. SMEDES
AUTHOR
HOW CAN IT BE ALL RIGHT WHEN EVERYTHING IS ALL WRONG?

WRAP-UP:

WHY IS FORGIVENESS DIFFICULT? WHY IS FORGIVING NOT THE SAME AS FORGETTING? WHAT ARE SOME STEPS TO TAKE IN THE FORGIVENESS PROCESS?

● ●

PROMISE 4: A MAN AND HIS FAMILY

MY RESPONSE AS A PROMISE KEEPER

Use this process for granting forgiveness:

1. Express it before the Lord first: "God, I forgive_____."

2. Then tell the individual you're forgiving: "I forgive you for _____

_____

_____."

3. Do it with God's grace: "I know I've done things like this myself. Let's agree to settle this and move on in our friendship."

THE REST OF THE STORY:

How can Pastor Everett be so forgiving? He explained, "I have known people whose loved ones had been murdered, and years afterward they still seemed consumed by anger and hatred. I didn't want that to happen to me."

Dress for Success?

• •

WARM-UP: STUDIES HAVE SHOWN THAT THOSE WHO DRESS IN A SUIT AND TIE IN OUR CULTURE ARE USUALLY THOUGHT OF AS MORE PROFESSIONAL, BETTER EQUIPPED FOR DECISION MAKING, AND MORE SUITED FOR RESPONSIBILITIES. WHAT WENT INTO THE DECISION TO DRESS AS YOU HAVE TODAY?

BACKGROUND

Today, so much attention is given to appearance, image, showmanship, media appeal, and sound bites. How often we are captured by someone's charismatic demeanor! In our culture, the outside of a man is generally the only measuring stick that people use to judge the person and his effective-ness. In 1 Samuel 16, we find a different measuring stick—the inside of a man. This session gives us insight into how God looked beyond the outside of a young man named David.

READ

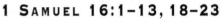

1 SAMUEL 16:1–13, 18–23

QUESTIONS FOR INTERACTION:

1 Why had God rejected Saul from being king over Israel? (see 1 Sam. 15:22-26)

2 Why do you think Samuel assumed Eliab was God's choice? (vv. 6-7)

3 What is the outside/inside controversy regarding the evaluation of a person?

4 How was David viewed by most who knew him?

CONSIDER THIS:

"FORGIVE US, LORD, FOR THE THINGS WE HAVE DONE THAT MAKE US UNCOMFORTABLE IN THY PRESENCE. ALL THE FRONT THAT WE POLISH SO CAREFULLY FOR MEN TO SEE, DOES NOT DECEIVE THEE."

PETER MARSHALL
PREACHER AND TEACHER

5 If you're in a management position, what should your yardstick for measuring leadership look like?

6 According to verse 12, why did God select David?

WRAP-UP: IF WE WISH TO DRESS FOR SUCCESS IN GOD'S EYES, WHAT SHOULD WE PUT ON? MAKE A LIST.

● ●

PROMISE 3: A MAN AND HIS INTEGRITY

MY RESPONSE AS A PROMISE KEEPER

I am surrounded by people in the marketplace who have dressed for success, and I realize I must dress appropriately for where I work.

I will, however, begin looking beyond the surface of my associates, as God does.

I won't put my trust in my own outward appearance but will focus on the importance of pleasing God within me.

Slaying Giants

P R O M I S E   7 :   A   M A N   A N D   H I S   W O R L D

EVERY EVENING'S NEWS PUTS GIANTS IN OUR FACES. WE WONDER WHAT WE CAN DO. WE CAN'T HELP BUT FEEL HELPLESS AND HOPELESS. WHAT GIANT ISSUES FACE OUR COMMUNITY/NATION REPORTED IN LAST NIGHT'S NEWS? IS THERE ANYTHING WE CAN DO AS MEN? IDEAS?

BACKGROUND

The story of David slaying Goliath is a classic for many reasons. Every one of us can identify with this story because we all face giants in our lives in one form or another. The giant looming down the valley could take the form of the neighborhood bully while growing up. But now it takes on new forms like debt, a supervisor, discouragement, loss of job, and problems at home. Let's see if we can gain insight on slaying our own giants.

READ

1 SAMUEL 17:1-54

QUESTIONS FOR INTERACTION:

❶ What's unusual in the way this battle was staged?

❷ What was so intimidating about this giant?

❸ What kind of shadow did Goliath cast over Israel? (vv. 8-11, 24, 32)

❹ In what ways was David prepared to face this giant?

PK PROMISE
K E E P E R S®
MEN OF INTEGRITY

5 Why was there low confidence in David's ability to kill Goliath?

6 What caused David to be so bold with the giant? (vv. 34-36)

7 What was the ripple effect in the land once the giant fell?

WRAP-UP: DAVID KEPT STUFFED LIONS AND BEARS IN HIS TROPHY CASE. WHAT IS THE VALUE OF REMEMBERING PAST VICTORIES? EACH MAN DESCRIBE ONE MAJOR GIANT THAT IS LOOMING LARGER THAN LIFE OVER HIM AT THIS TIME.

● ●

PROMISE 7: A MAN AND HIS WORLD

MY RESPONSE AS A PROMISE KEEPER

Not one of David's countrymen came alongside him in battle. As Promise Keepers, we can encourage each other before, during, and after battles.

I will make it a point to pray immediately when I see a giant threatening.

BRIDGE OVER TROUBLED BORDERS

PROMISE 6: A MAN AND HIS BROTHERS

●●●

WARM-UP: RACIAL TENSIONS HAD BEEN SMOLDERING FOR YEARS IN LOS ANGELES BETWEEN MANY ETHNIC GROUPS. IN THE MIDST OF THE FIERY L.A. RIOTS OF 1992, AN IMPASSIONED RODNEY KING CRIED OUT TO HIS CITY, "CAN'T WE ALL JUST GET ALONG?" WHAT PREVENTS A CITY LIKE LOS ANGELES FROM "GETTING ALONG"? IN AN INTERRACIAL CULTURE, WHAT STRUGGLES DO YOU HAVE? WHAT RACIAL SLURS BOTHER YOU? WHY?

BACKGROUND

The reason for hostility between the Jews and the Samaritans goes back a long way. When the Jews returned from exile in Babylon, the Samaritans offered to help them rebuild their temple, but the offer was refused. This naturally engendered great bitterness. The Samaritans refused to worship at Jerusalem, the Jews later (128 B.C.) burned the Samaritans' temple on Mount Gerizan, and harsh relations between the two groups became widespread.

READ

JOHN 4:1–19, 29–30, 39

QUESTIONS FOR INTERACTION:

1 Given the racial tensions existing between the Jews and the Samaritans, why would Jesus want to travel through Samaria?

2 What did He do to cross the barrier of racial/ethnic tension?

3 Prejudice defined: "A judgment or opinion formed before the facts are known." What situations seem to arouse prejudice in us?

4 What gave Jesus the freedom to talk with the woman at the well about her personal life?

5 How did the Samaritan woman open the racial borders?

WRAP-UP:

GO AROUND THE GROUP AND ANSWER THIS QUESTION: "WHAT GIVES SOMEONE THE FREEDOM TO TALK TO YOU ABOUT YOUR PERSONAL LIFE, EVEN TO THE POINT OF POSSIBLY POINTING OUT PREJUDICE?"

● ●

PROMISE 6: A MAN AND HIS BROTHERS

CONSIDER THIS:

STAN MET RACHEL AT THE UNIVERSITY OF NEBRASKA. HIS FOOTBALL CAREER AT NEBRASKA WAS BEING APPLAUDED THROUGHOUT THE BIG 8 AND BEYOND. RACHEL'S FATHER, HOWEVER, HAD TO DEAL WITH MUCH MORE THAN CELEBRITY STATUS FOR HIS DAUGHTER WHEN CONFRONTED BY THE REALITY OF AN INTERRACIAL MARRIAGE. THIS WAS ALTOGETHER NEW TO THIS FAMILY. FOLLOWING NEARLY SIX MONTHS OF PRAYER AND PER-SONAL EVALUATION, THIS DAD'S ANSWER TO STAN'S REQUEST TO MARRY HIS DAUGHTER WAS THIS: "STAN, GOD HAS BEEN SAY-ING TO ME, 'I'M GIVING YOU A GIFT, EVERYTHING YOU EVER WANTED IN A SON-IN-LAW. ARE YOU GOING TO GIVE IT BACK TO ME BECAUSE IT DIDN'T COME IN THE WRAPPING YOU THOUGHT IT WOULD BE WRAPPED IN?"

MY RESPONSE AS A PROMISE KEEPER

When do I tend to have the most prejudice?_____

_____

_____

_____

What interracial bridge can I help build in my church and community?_____

_____

_____

_____

INCREDIBLE POWER

●●

WARM-UP: SOME YEARS AGO IN LIFE MAGAZINE, THERE APPEARED A FULL-PAGE PICTURE OF THE DEVASTATION WROUGHT BY A MIDWESTERN TORNADO. IN THE CENTER OF THE PHOTO WAS A TELEPHONE POLE WITH A STRAW DRIVEN THROUGH IT. IT SEEMED INCREDIBLE. HOW COULD A WEAK AND FRAGILE STRAW BE THRUST THROUGH A RUGGED, SEASONED TELE-PHONE POLE? THE ANSWER: THE STRAW, WHICH HAS NO POWER OF ITS OWN, HAD BEEN EMPOWERED TOTALLY BY THE AWESOME FORCE OF THE TORNADO. MOTHER TERESA, ONE OF GOD'S "STRAWS" IN THIS WORLD, HAS PENETRATED THE LIVES OF COUNTLESS THOUSANDS OF PEOPLE. HOW DO YOU EXPLAIN THE POWER DISPLAYED AROUND THE WORLD BY THIS FRAGILE AND SEEMINGLY INSIGNIFICANT SISTER OF CHARITY?

BACKGROUND

In the session "Power to Change," we saw Peter's remarkable shift from being easily intimidated to being a person of outspoken confidence. The only way to explain this transformation is by the activity of the Holy Spirit in him. Today we continue the story of Peter and John in the marketplace of Jerusalem. Jesus had recently ascended, and His promised power was fully displayed within these two men.

READ

ACTS 1:6–9

QUESTIONS FOR INTERACTION:

1 Why do you think Jesus sensed His disciples need-ed power as He gave them His last few words?

2 What kind of witness might the disciples have given without the Holy Spirit?

PROMISE KEEPERS
MEN OF INTEGRITY

CONSIDER THIS:

"THE GREAT DIFFERENCE BETWEEN PRESENT-DAY CHRISTIANITY AND THAT OF WHICH WE READ IN THESE LETTERS [NEW TESTAMENT EPISTLES] IS THAT TO US, IT IS PRIMARILY A PERFOR-MANCE; TO THEM IT WAS A REAL EXPERIENCE. WE ARE APT TO REDUCE THE CHRISTIAN RELIGION TO A CODE OR, AT BEST, A RULE OF HEART AND LIFE."

J.B. PHILLIPS
AUTHOR
THE NEW TESTAMENT IN MODERN ENGLISH

3 What kind of witness did Peter and John give with the power of the Holy Spirit?

4 If you were arrested for talking about Christ in your workplace, what do you think the Spirit of God would lead you to say in your defense?

5 How did the Holy Spirit lead Peter and John to respond to the resistance of the religious leaders?

6 What results were seen in the witnesses when they were empowered by the Holy Spirit? (see v. 31)

WRAP-UP. FINISH THIS SENTENCE: I WILL PRAY FOR BOLDNESS IN MY WITNESS TO _____ AND TRUST THAT GOD'S POWER WILL BE AT WORK. NOW TELL THE OTHER MEN WHOSE NAME YOU WROTE DOWN.

• •

PROMISE 7: A MAN AND HIS WORLD

MY RESPONSE AS A PROMISE KEEPER

Listed are the names of three people I want to see come to Christ. I will look for opportunities to be a witness to them: _____

_____ .

BODY BUILDING

● ●

WARM-UP:

A WINNING TEAM IS BUILT BY THE EFFORTS OF ALL ITS MEMBERS. THE TRAINERS IN THE WEIGHT ROOM, THE COACHING STAFF, AND THE PERSONNEL IN THE FRONT OFFICE ARE AS MUCH A PART OF THE VICTORY ON SUNDAY AFTERNOON AS THE JERRY RICES WHO SCRAMBLE FOR TDS. WHY DO YOU SUPPOSE SOME CONSIDER THE 1994 SAN FRANCISCO '49ERS TO BE THE BEST TEAM EVER TO PLAY IN A SUPER BOWL?

BACKGROUND

In today's passage, the apostle Paul spoke to the all-important issue of the church. Specifically, he addressed the roles and responsibilities of its "coaches" and "players." Each church member does not seek his own betterment, but rather the development of the whole body, in order for the church to "win." Increasing the size of the church is not of primary importance in this context. Rather, the goal is to mentor its members in spiritual growth.

READ

EPHESIANS 4:11–16

QUESTIONS FOR INTERACTION:

❶ What are the responsibilities of church leaders?

❷ What are the measurements of a full-grown church? (v. 13)

❸ What are the measurements of a childish church?

4 How does a church progress toward maturity? (v. 15)

5 How can you help bring spiritual maturity to your church?

6 Why must every member contribute to the growth of the church?

WRAP-UP: THE CHURCH IS CLEARLY A VITAL PART OF GOD'S PLAN FOR OUR LIVES. HOW CAN YOU HELP IT TO GROW, BOTH INDIVIDUALLY AND AS A GROUP OF PROMISE KEEPERS?

• •

PROMISE 5: A MAN AND HIS CHURCH

MY RESPONSE AS A PROMISE KEEPER

This next Sunday, I will express appreciation to one of my church's leaders.

His/her name: _____

I will prayerfully consider how I can be involved in being equipped by or helping to equip fellow members, beginning with my own family.

EYES UP, KNEES DOWN

PROMISE 1: A MAN AND HIS GOD

• •

BACKGROUND

Israel was captive in Babylon. Obviously, the nation was discouraged. God used the prophet Isaiah to renew Israel's perspective by telling the people that God is greater than their former sins, their difficult circumstances, and their feelings of despair.

READ

ISAIAH 40:12–17

QUESTIONS FOR INTERACTION:

1 Why did Isaiah want Israel to grasp the grandeur of God's greatness?

2 What are the measurements of His greatness?

READ

ISAIAH 40:18–26

3 Why do people build idols? What are they?

PROMISE KEEPERS®
MEN OF INTEGRITY

4 Why is faith in an idol so preposterous?

90

5 Why was reading this message from Isaiah the first step toward freedom for a captive Israel?

READ

ISAIAH 40:27–31

6 In light of God's greatness, what does real freedom look like?

7 What must we do to bring God's strength to bear on our weakness?

WRAP-UP. WHAT DOES IT MEAN TO "WAIT ON THE LORD"? AS A GROUP, TAKE A FEW MINUTES TO PRAY TOGETHER AND RENEW PERSPECTIVE, USING THE VERSES OF OUR STUDY AS THE CONTENT OF YOUR PRAYERS.

AS WE APPROACH THE END OF OUR YEAR OF STUDY, WHERE IS OUR GROUP ON THE RELATIONAL DIAMOND DESCRIBED ON PAGES 11–12? HAVE WE MADE NOTICEABLE PROGRESS TOWARD BROTHERHOOD AND CHRISTLIKENESS? HOW CAN WE KEEP OUR RELATIONSHIPS GROWING? (PART OF THE ANSWER MAY BE TO CONTINUE WITH THE NEXT PROMISE BUILDERS STUDY GUIDE, THE PROMISE KEEPER AT WORK.)

● ●

PROMISE 1: A MAN AND HIS GOD

MY RESPONSE AS A PROMISE KEEPER

The next time I feel discouraged, my first step will be to read Isaiah 40.

My next step will be to get my eyes up and my knees down.

PASS THE SALT, PLEASE

PROMISE 7: A MAN AND HIS WORLD

• •

WARM-UP: IT IS AUGUST IN ATLANTA—THE TEMPERATURE AND HUMIDITY ARE **98** AND **98**, AND NO BREEZE. THE AC IS OUT IN YOUR CIVIC, YOU'RE DRESSED TO VISIT YOUR BANKER, AND YOU NEED A THIRST-QUENCHER. IT'S TIME TO STOP FOR A COKE. WHAT DO YOU ENJOY ABOUT A LARGE COKE ON A HOT DAY? WHAT DO YOU DO WITH A COKE THAT HAS LOST ITS FIZZ?

BACKGROUND

As the master teacher, Jesus had the ability to take the basic things of life and fill them with life-changing meaning. Today's short passage is a classic study of challenging the common-place. Don't be fooled by its simplicity.

READ

MATTHEW 5:13

QUESTIONS FOR INTERACTION:

1 From what you've heard or read, how significant was salt in Jesus' day?

2 Since you are the salt, what are you to do?

3 What could weaken your effectiveness as salt?

4 How can we help each other stay salty?

5 From what you've heard or read, how significant was a lamp in Jesus' day?

6 Since you are the light, what are you to do?

7 What could weaken your effectiveness as light?

8 How can we help each other keep our lights shining?

WRAP-UP: GOD GIVES US TO A CULTURE VOID OF TASTE AND MEANING. WE ARE HIS SALT AND HIS LIGHT. WE HAVE INCREDIBLE SIGNIFICANCE. AS A GROUP, PAUSE AND PRAISE HIM FOR FILLING OUR SHAKERS AND FUELING OUR LAMPS.

PROMISE 7: A MAN AND HIS WORLD

MY RESPONSE AS A PROMISE KEEPER

Here are some ways I can be salt and light in my workplace this week: _____

_____

_____.

I will begin praying for five men to attend an upcoming Promise Keepers men's conference, and for men who will begin a new Promise Keepers group with me.

THANKS!

PROMISE 4: A MAN AND HIS FAMILY

WARM-UP: THANKSGIVING DAY IS A FAVORITE FOR MOST MEN—NO UNDUE COMMERCIALISM, NOTHING TO OUTDO FROM LAST YEAR, NO LAST-MINUTE SHOPPING, THE DALLAS COWBOYS IN THE AFTERNOON, AND JUST ENOUGH TRADITION TO REKINDLE GREAT MEMORIES OF FAMILIES TOGETHER, GIVING THANKS.

WHAT IS A FAVORITE MEMORY OF PAST THANKSGIVINGS? WHAT'S THE VALUE OF BEING GRATEFUL?

BACKGROUND

Psalm 107 was originally composed for use at one of Israel's annual religious festivals. This psalm calls us to give thanks to the Lord for His wonderful deliverance from over-whelming circumstances. It instructs us in the wisdom of seeing the loving hand of God in our sufferings, moving us once again to a place of safety and praise to Him.

READ

PSALM 107:1-3

QUESTIONS FOR INTERACTION:

❶ Why does the Lord call us to be grateful to Him?

❷ What is profound about describing the Lord as simply good (as contrasted with super, incredible, fantastic, unbelievable)?

READ

PSALM 107:4-9

❸ What situation caused distress for these people?

PROMISE
KEEPERS®
MEN OF INTEGRITY

4 How did their difficult circumstances help bring them to a place of thanksgiving?

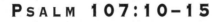

READ
PSALM 107:10–15

5 What situation caused distress for these people?

6 How did their difficult circumstances help bring them to a place of thanksgiving?

WRAP-UP: WHAT HAPPENS TO MEN WHO STOP BEING THANKFUL? EACH MAN EXPRESS THANKS FOR ONE THING IN PRAYER.

• •

PROMISE 4: A MAN AND HIS FAMILY

MY RESPONSE AS A PROMISE KEEPER

I will commit to lead my family this Thanksgiving to remember some highlights of His goodness to us in this past year. (Suggestion: when the family is together for a meal) _____

_____

_____

_____

_____

A "MARY, MARY" OR A "MARTHA, MARTHA" CHRISTMAS?

PROMISE 1: A MAN AND HIS GOD

● ●

WARM-UP.

WHAT HAVE YOU DONE TO GET READY FOR CHRISTMAS? HOW WOULD YOUR SPOUSE OR FRIENDS DESCRIBE YOU DURING THIS HOLIDAY?

BACKGROUND

What we're like during the busy Christmas season is the result of what has our attention. Jesus was wrapping up His busiest day recorded in the Bible and had been welcomed into the home of friends. This home, some two miles from the rush of Jerusalem, had become a place of frequent restful visits for Him. These five sentences from Dr. Luke's account are loaded with insight for us during this busiest of all seasons.

READ

LUKE 10:38–42

QUESTIONS FOR INTERACTION:

1 Why do you think each of these sisters had such a different focus?

2 What words would best describe each of them as they celebrated the Lord's presence?

3 What do you suppose Jesus meant when He said, "Only a few things are necessary, really only one"?

4 What did Mary choose that "shall not be taken away from her"?

5 Jesus, out of increasing public pressure, retreated again to this home about a week before His death. What can we learn about valuing the Lord's presence from the three Bethany hosts in John's account? (John 11:54–12:8)

WRAP-UP. DO YOU PREDICT YOURS TO BE A "MARY, MARY" OR A "MARTHA, MARTHA" CHRISTMAS? WHY?

● ●

PROMISE 1: A MAN AND HIS GOD

MY RESPONSE AS A PROMISE KEEPER

This tale of two sisters appears to be an issue of the eyes, of focus, of perspective. In what area do I need fresh perspective this season?

_____

_____

_____

_____

_____

LOOKING BACK AND LOOKING FORWARD

PROMISE 7: A MAN AND HIS WORLD

· ·

WARM-UP: IN THE PASSING OF 12 MONTHS, IT'S AMAZING HOW MUCH HAPPENS IN OUR LIVES. FOR EXAMPLE, IT MAY BE DIFFICULT TO CHOOSE THE TOP 10 NEWS STORIES OF THE PAST YEAR FROM THE MANY POSSIBILITIES. LOOKING BACK, WHAT TOP TWO NEWS EVENTS WILL YOU REMEMBER FROM THIS PAST YEAR (GLOBAL, LOCAL, ATHLETICS, FINANCIAL)?

BACKGROUND

It is the grace of God to measure our lifetime in terms of years. As one year ends and a new one begins, it is the perfect time to take stock of our lives. We do well to reflect on where we've been and to set some goals for the new year just ahead. It's almost like magic to see how our lives improve with the wisdom of looking back and the challenge of looking forward.

READ

PSALM 90

QUESTIONS FOR INTERACTION:

1 What have been two highlights of this past year?

2 What have you seen God do in your life during the year?

3 What has been your most difficult experience? What did you learn from it?

PROMISE KEEPERS®
MEN OF INTEGRITY

4 What have you learned about family relationships that should benefit you in the coming year?

5 What do we learn about the character of God from Moses in Psalm 90?

WRAP-UP: IN WHAT WAYS DOES A FRESH UNDERSTANDING OF THE CHARACTER OF GOD GIVE US HOPE FOR THE NEW YEAR? WHAT WOULD EACH OF US LIKE GOD TO DO IN OUR GROUP IN THE NEXT YEAR?

• •

PROMISE 7: A MAN AND HIS WORLD

MY RESPONSE AS A PROMISE KEEPER

What are two or three goals I am setting for the new year?_____

_____

_____

_____

What would I like God to do in *me* in this new year?_____

_____

_____

_____

_____

PLANS AND PROMISES FOR THE NEW YEAR

PROMISE 3: A MAN AND HIS INTEGRITY

WARM-UP. ON THE EVENING FOLLOWING THIS PROMISE BUILDER SESSION, RALPH LEANED ACROSS THE DINNER TABLE WITH THIS REQUEST OF HIS WIFE: "HONEY, WHAT IS THE CHANCE WE CAN EXTEND THE DESSERT TONIGHT, JUST THE TWO OF US? I FEEL WE NEED TO DO SOME PLANNING TOGETHER FOR THIS NEW YEAR!" HIS WIFE'S LAST AUDIBLE SOUND BEFORE SLIPPING INTO SHOCK WAS THIS: "I AM SO THRILLED THAT THE TWO OF US ARE GOING TO DO SOME PLANNING!"

WHAT ARE THE UPSIDES OF PLANNING? WHAT ARE THE DOWNSIDES OF PLANNING?

BACKGROUND

Promises are not likely to be kept without a plan. And plans are no better than the promises behind them. Most of us know, however, that there are great benefits from both. "We should make plans—counting on God to direct us" (Prov. 16:9, LB).

READ

PROVERBS 16:9 (LB)

QUESTIONS FOR INTERACTION:

❶ What is our part and what is God's part in the planning process?

❷ Without looking ahead to the Personal Planning Worksheet, discuss what areas of our lives need to be planned.

❸ Rank the above areas in order of importance. Talk about why you selected your order.

PROMISE
KEEPERS®
MEN OF INTEGRITY

TURN TO THE PERSONAL PLANNING WORKSHEET, AND GET STARTED BY DISCUSSING AS A GROUP SOME PRACTICAL IDEAS FOR EACH OF THE CATEGORIES.

CONSIDER THIS:

TO FAIL TO PLAN IS TO PLAN TO FAIL.

• •

PROMISE 3: A MAN AND HIS INTEGRITY

MY RESPONSE AS A PROMISE KEEPER

Within the next three weeks, by _____(date), I will sit down with my wife and together complete this Personal Planning Worksheet.

PERSONAL PLANNING WORKSHEET

"We should make plans—counting on God to direct us" (Prov. 16:9, LB).
What would we like to accomplish by the end of this year?

	PLANS	RESOURCES NEEDED
with work		
with the church		
with the Lord		
for myself		
for our marriage		
with ministry in the workplace		
with the family		
in our friendships		
in our community		

Note: The above are not listed in any priority order.

GHOSTS

PROMISE 1: A MAN AND HIS GOD

••

WARM-UP. ANY NUMBER OF FILMS DEAL WITH THE TOPIC OF PEOPLE COMING
BACK FROM THE DEAD: A FOOTBALL PLAYER CAME BACK TO LIFE TO
LEAD HIS TEAM TO VICTORY; A BUSINESSMAN RETURNED FROM DEATH
TO RESCUE HIS WIFE FROM A BAD SECOND MARRIAGE; A YOUNG LION
WAS ENCOURAGED TO RESTORE THE KINGDOM AFTER HIS DECEASED
FATHER MADE AN APPEARANCE.

WHY DO VIEWERS HAVE SUCH FASCINATION WITH THOSE COMING BACK
FROM THE DEAD?

BACKGROUND

The apostle Paul placed
the resurrection of Jesus
Christ at the very foundation of the Christian's faith.
Even though that resurrection is the best-attested
fact of ancient history, the
church at Corinth needed
reassurance that His resurrection was both factual
and critical to its faith.

READ

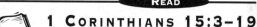

1 CORINTHIANS 15:3–19

QUESTIONS FOR INTERACTION:

1 What is the historical reality of the resurrection?

2 What difference would it make to Christianity if
Christ had not been raised from the dead?

3 What difference would it make to you if Christ
had not been raised from the dead?

PROMISE
KEEPERS®
MEN OF INTEGRITY

1 CORINTHIANS 15:50–58

CONSIDER THIS:

"AFTER MORE THAN 700 HOURS OF STUDYING THIS SUBJECT, AND THOROUGHLY INVESTIGATING ITS FOUNDATION, I HAVE COME TO THE CONCLUSION THAT THE RESURRECTION OF JESUS CHRIST IS EITHER ONE OF THE 'MOST WICKED, VICIOUS, HEARTLESS HOAXES EVER FOISTED UPON THE MINDS OF MEN, OR IT IS THE MOST FANTASTIC FACT OF HISTORY.'"

JOSH MCDOWELL
AUTHOR AND SPEAKER
EVIDENCE THAT DEMANDS A VERDICT

4 What confidence do we have that when we die we will also be raised?

5 What is there about work (toil) that makes it futile, empty, vain? How can reflecting on the resurrection of Jesus affect our view of work?

WRAP-UP: DESCRIBE HOW THE LIVING CHRIST HAS CHANGED YOUR LIFE. (EACH MAN TAKE ONLY ONE MINUTE.)

●●

PROMISE 1: A MAN AND HIS GOD

MY RESPONSE AS A PROMISE KEEPER

I will read the resurrection story with my family sometime during this Easter week.

I will look for opportunities this week to talk about the real meaning of Easter with someone in my workplace.

PROMISE BUILDERS

PRAYER JOURNAL

DATE	PRAYER REQUEST	FROM	ANSWER

PROMISE BUILDERS

DATE	PRAYER REQUEST	FROM	ANSWER

PROMISE BUILDERS

PRAYER JOURNAL

DATE	PRAYER REQUEST	FROM	ANSWER

PROMISE BUILDERS

PRAYER JOURNAL

DATE	PRAYER REQUEST	FROM	ANSWER

PROMISE BUILDERS

PRAYER JOURNAL

DATE	PRAYER REQUEST	FROM	ANSWER

PROMISE BUILDERS

PRAYER JOURNAL

DATE	PRAYER REQUEST	FROM	ANSWER

PROMISE BUILDERS

(Make photocopies of this page if you need more prayer journal space.)

PRAYER JOURNAL

DATE	PRAYER REQUEST	FROM	ANSWER

ADDITIONAL RESOURCES

AVAILABLE FROM PROMISE KEEPERS

PERIODICALS & STUDY TOOLS

THE POWER OF A PROMISE KEPT
Gregg Lewis (Colorado Springs, Colo.: Focus on the Family, 1995)

SEVEN PROMISES OF A PROMISE KEEPER
(Colorado Springs, Colo.: Focus on the Family, 1994)
Also available on four 90-minute audiocassettes.

PROMISE BUILDERS STUDY SERIES: THE PROMISE KEEPER AT WORK
Bob Horner, Ron Ralston, David Sunde
(Colorado Springs, Colo.: Focus on the Family, 1996)

STRATEGIES FOR A SUCCESSFUL MARRIAGE: A STUDY GUIDE FOR MEN
E. Glenn Wagner, Ph.D. (Colorado Springs, Colo.: NavPress, 1994)

FOCUSING YOUR MEN'S MINISTRY
Peter A. Richardson (Denver: Promise Keepers, 1993)

BROTHERS! CALLING MEN INTO VITAL RELATIONSHIPS
Geoff Gorsuch and Dan Schaffer (Denver: Promise Keepers, 1993)

DAILY DISCIPLINES FOR THE CHRISTIAN MAN
Bob Beltz (Colorado Springs, Colo.: NavPress, 1993)

WHAT GOD DOES WHEN MEN PRAY
William Carr Peel (Colorado Springs, Colo.: NavPress, 1993)

WHAT IS A PROMISE KEEPER?
(Denver: Promise Keepers, 1993)
Available in audiocassette only.

WHAT MAKES A MAN? & STUDY GUIDE
Bill McCartney (Colorado Springs, Colo.: NavPress, 1992)

WORSHIP & PRAISE MUSIC

RAISE THE STANDARD
Maranatha! Music (Laguna Hills, Calif.: 1995)
Available in: Compact Disc
                 Audiocassette

PK LIVE: WORSHIP TAPE
Maranatha! Music (Laguna Hills, Calif.: 1994)
Available in: Compact Disc
                 Audiocassette

SEIZE THE MOMENT: WORSHIP FOR MEN
Maranatha! Music (Laguna Hills, Calif.: 1994)
Available in: Compact Disc
                 Audiocassette

PROMISE KEEPERS: A LIFE THAT SHOWS
Sparrow (Brentwood, Tenn.: 1994)
Available in: Compact Disc
                 Audiocassette
                 Songbook

FACE TO FACE: WORSHIP FOR MEN
Maranatha! Music (Laguna Hills, Calif.: 1993)
Available in: Compact Disc
                 Audiocassette
                 Songbook
                 Words Only

FOR ADDITIONAL INFORMATION AND RESOURCES
Call: 1-800-456-7594
Or write to: Promise Keepers
P.O. Box 18376
Boulder, CO 80308